Grammar 3 Teacher's Book

Teaching grammar, spelling, and punctuation with the
Grammar 3 Student Book

Written by

Sara Wernham and Sue Lloyd

Edited by Louise Van-Pottelsberghe

Contents

PART 1:   THE GRAMMAR PROGRAM

Introduction   3

Teaching Ideas for Grammar   5

Teaching Ideas for Spelling   19

Spelling and Grammar Lessons   26

PART 2:   LESSON PLANS

Teaching with the Grammar 3 Student Book   31

Introduction

For ease of use, this *Teacher's Book* has been divided into two distinct parts. The first part gives a comprehensive introduction, which explains the teaching method in detail. It is a good idea to read this part of the *Teacher's Book* before using the *Grammar 3 Student and Teacher's Books* in the classroom. The second part of the *Teacher's Book* provides a thorough and structured lesson plan for each day of teaching. The lesson plans in this part of the book are designed specifically for use with the corresponding pages in the *Grammar 3 Student Book*.

The *Grammar 3 Student and Teacher's Books* are designed to follow on from the *Grammar 1* and *Grammar 2 Student and Teacher's Books*. They are intended to:

- extend and refine the students' understanding of the grammar already taught,
- introduce new elements of grammar,
- teach new spelling patterns systematically,
- develop dictionary and thesaurus skills,
- improve vocabulary and comprehension, and
- reinforce the teaching in the *Grammar 1* and *Grammar 2 Student and Teacher's Books*.

Like the activities in the previous *Student Books*, the teaching in the *Grammar 3 Student Book* is multisensory and active. In the *Grammar 3 Student Book*, particular emphasis is placed on consolidating the students' learning and helping them to apply their new skills. As before in the *Grammar 1* and *2 Student Books*, each part of speech is taught with an accompanying action and color. The actions not only enliven the teaching, but also make the parts of speech easier for the students to remember. The colors, which are useful when identifying and labeling parts of speech in sentences, are the same as those used in Montessori Schools.

As with previous *Teacher's Books*, the *Grammar 3 Teacher's Book* explains all the essential teaching ideas.

Students' Achievement

The most dramatic improvements to result from using the *Grammar 3 Student and Teacher's Books* will be found in the students' writing. After completing the *Grammar 3 Student Book*, the students will spell and punctuate more accurately, use a wider vocabulary, and have a clearer understanding of how language works.

In their first year at school, the *Phonics Student Books* taught the students to write independently by listening for the sounds in words and choosing letters to represent those sounds. This enables the students to write pages of news and stories. It is a joy to read their work and to see the great pride and confidence they derive from their newly acquired skills. It is important to build on this foundation in the following years. The *Grammar Student and Teacher's Books* provide teaching ideas designed to develop the students' writing skills. The students become more aware that they are writing for a purpose: that their words are intended to be read and understood. They learn that their writing is easier to understand if it is grammatically correct, accurately spelled, well punctuated, and neatly written. The students also learn that, if they use interesting words, their writing can give real pleasure. Even in the early stages, it is valuable for the students to have a simple understanding of this long-term goal.

The Format of the Student and Teacher's Books

The program for *Grammar 3* consists of a *Teacher's Book*, offering detailed lesson plans, and a corresponding *Student Book*, with activities for each lesson. Enough material is provided in these books for 36 weeks' teaching, with two lessons for each week. The *Grammar 3 Student Book* is designed so that there is one activity page for each lesson. Each lesson is intended to take up about one hour's teaching time.

Although it is referred to as the *Jolly Phonics* grammar program, there are in fact two elements, namely spelling and grammar. The material in the *Student and Teacher's Books* is organized so that the first of the week's lessons concentrates on spelling and the second on grammar. However, the terms are used loosely and there is some overlap: punctuation, vocabulary development, and dictionary work are among the areas covered in both spelling and grammar lessons. This is deliberate, as the two elements complement each other when combined.

The *Grammar 3* program covers the more structured aspects of literacy, and is intended to take up only part of the teaching time set aside for literacy work. If two days' literacy lessons are devoted to *Grammar 3* each week, this leaves three lessons that can be devoted to the areas not covered by *Grammar 3*, such as comprehension, group and individual reading, formal and creative writing, and handwriting practice. The students should be shown how spelling and grammar relate to their other literacy work. For instance, if the students have recently learned about contractions, and there is an example of one in the text they are studying, they can be encouraged to spot it and to identify which letter(s) the apostrophe is replacing.

For each activity page in the *Student Book* there is a corresponding page in the *Teacher's Book*, offering a detailed lesson plan and useful teaching guidance. More detailed explanations and advice are provided in the two following sections: *Teaching Ideas for Grammar* and *Teaching Ideas for Spelling*. Relevant material from the *Grammar 1* and *2 Teacher's Books* has also been included for easy reference.

To avoid confusion, the *Jolly Phonics* materials follow the convention of using different parentheses to distinguish between letter names and letter sounds. Letter names are shown between these parentheses: ‹ ›. For example, the word *ship* begins with the letter ‹s›. By contrast, letter sounds are shown between these parentheses: / /. For example, the word *ship* begins with the /sh/ sound.

Teaching Ideas for Grammar

The benefits of learning grammar are cumulative. In the early stages, the students' grammar knowledge will help them to improve the clarity and quality of their writing. Later on, their grammar knowledge will help them to understand more complicated texts, learn foreign languages with greater ease, and use Standard English in their speech and writing.

The accents and dialects in spoken English vary from region to region. The grammar we learn first is picked up through our speech and varies accordingly. However, at times, there is a need for uniformity. If we all follow the same linguistic conventions, communication throughout the English-speaking world is greatly improved. An awareness of this fact helps those students who do not speak Standard English to understand that the way they speak is not wrong, but that it has not been chosen as the standard for the whole country. All students need to learn the standard form of English, as well as appreciating their own dialect.

In their first two years of *Grammar*, the students were introduced to the concepts of sentences, punctuation, and parts of speech. In the *Grammar 1 Student Book*, they learned about proper and common nouns, pronouns, verbs, adjectives, and adverbs, and they learned to use verbs to indicate whether something happened in the past, present, or future. In the *Grammar 2 Student Book*, the students' knowledge was extended and their understanding deepened. Their knowledge of sentences was refined and they learned to punctuate with greater variety and precision. They were also introduced to irregular verbs and to new parts of speech, namely possessive adjectives, conjunctions, prepositions, and comparative and superlative adjectives.

In the *Grammar 3 Student Book*, the students' understanding is further refined. They learn how to distinguish between a phrase and a sentence, how to identify the subject and object of a sentence, and how to organize sentences into paragraphs. The students also learn how to form the continuous tenses and are introduced to new parts of speech, namely collective nouns, irregular plurals, possessive pronouns, and object pronouns. In dictation, they receive regular practice in writing direct speech with the proper punctuation. They also have regular dictionary and parsing practice with the aim of building their dictionary skills, improving their vocabulary, and reinforcing their grammar knowledge.

The *Grammar 3 Student Book* builds upon the teaching in the *Grammar 1* and *Grammar 2 Student Books*, so the students' understanding of this teaching must be secure before moving on. For this reason, it is important to go over anything the students are unsure of before introducing anything new. The *Grammar Student Books* provide a systematic approach to learning. This enables even the slowest learners to keep up, while ensuring that more able students master their skills thoroughly and develop good grammatical habits. Every lesson should include a review session. Suggestions are provided in the lesson plans, but teachers should feel free to use their own judgment when deciding which areas their students need to revisit.

The term *grammar* is used quite broadly with students of this age. Definitions of the parts of speech, and of what constitutes a sentence, have necessarily been simplified to age-appropriate working definitions. As the students grow older, these definitions can be expanded and refined.

Nouns

A noun denotes a person, place, or thing. On the most basic level, nouns can be divided into proper nouns and common nouns.

Proper Nouns

Proper nouns were introduced in the *Grammar 1 Student Book* and reviewed in the *Grammar 2 Student Book*. The students learned that a proper noun starts with a capital letter, and is the particular name given to the following:

Action: The action for a **proper noun** is to touch one's forehead with the index and middle fingers.

Color: The color for all types of noun is black.

- a person, including that person's last name and title,
- a place, for example a river, mountain, park, street, town, country, continent, or planet,
- a building, for example a school, house, library, swimming pool, or theater,
- a date, for example a day of the week, a month, or a religious holiday.

In the *Grammar 1 Student Book* the main focus was on people's names being proper nouns. In the *Grammar 2 Student Book* the names of the months, including their correct spelling and sequence, were the focus. In the *Grammar 3 Student Book* the focus moves to place names. The students learn that in longer place names, such as the *Tower of London*, only the important words need a capital letter, not the short joining words.

Common Nouns

All nouns that are not specific names or titles are called common nouns. Common nouns can be further divided into concrete nouns (e.g. *table* or *child*), abstract nouns (e.g. *beauty* or *kindness*), and collective nouns (e.g. the **class** or a **flock** of birds). Although there are three types of common

Action: The action for a **common noun** is to touch one's forehead with all the fingers of one hand.

Color: The color for all types of noun is black.

noun, only concrete nouns are taught in the early stages. The intangible nature of abstract nouns, like *happiness*, means that they are difficult for young students to grasp.

Everything we can see has a name by which we can refer to it, for example *table*, *chair*, and *pencil*. As these names are not specific to any one object, but refer to tables, chairs, and so on in general, they are called common nouns and not proper nouns. At this stage the students find it useful to think of nouns as the names for things they can see and touch. A good way to help the students decide if a word is a noun is to encourage them to say *a, an,* or *the* before the word and see whether it makes sense. For example, *a chair, an elephant,* and *the table* make sense, whereas *a fell, an unhappy,* and *the ran* do not. (The words *a, an,* and *the* are the three articles, and are explained later.)

In general, students understand the concept of nouns easily and have no trouble when asked to think of examples. Despite this, it can still be difficult for them to identify nouns in written sentences. This becomes easier with regular parsing practice, which is provided at the bottom of the spelling pages in the *Grammar 3 Student Book.*

Collective Nouns

In the *Grammar 3 Student Book*, collective nouns are introduced. Collective nouns are words used to describe groups of people, animals, or things: for example, *a **crowd** of people, a **herd** of cows,* or *a **fleet** of ships*. Collective nouns can also describe groups of abstract nouns: for example, *a **host** of ideas* or *a **wash** of emotions*, but these are only introduced when the students are old enough to understand abstract nouns.

Collective nouns are usually singular (e.g. *a bunch, a band, a flock*) because they describe the group as a whole; whereas the nouns that make up the group are plural (e.g. *a bunch of **flowers**, a band of **robbers**, a flock of **birds***) because there are many of them. Collective nouns are a type of common noun, so they do not need a capital letter. Often, the same collective noun can be used to describe a number of different things; for example, *bunch* can be used to describe, among other things, flowers, keys, and bananas. Sometimes more than one collective noun can be used to describe the same item; for example, a group of whales can be described as *a pod* or *a school*. Many collective nouns are used to describe groups of animals and birds. Some are very common (e.g. *herd, flock, pride*), while others, particularly those used for birds, are quite obscure (e.g. *a **murder** of crows*). Many new collective nouns, like *a **bounce** of kangaroos*, are not officially recognized, but are nevertheless entertaining for the students.

It is important not to confuse collective nouns with uncountable nouns. Uncountable nouns, such as *furniture, water,* and *meat*, are almost always singular. Collective nouns, on the other hand, can be referred to in the plural when they describe more than one group of a particular type of object (e.g. *two **colonies** of ants*).

Plurals

Most nouns change in the plural, that is, when they describe more than one. In the *Grammar 1 and 2 Student Books,* the two main ways of forming the plural were introduced: adding ‹-s› to the noun (as in *dogs* and *boys*), and adding ‹-es› to those nouns that end with ‹sh›, ‹ch›, ‹s›, ‹z›, or ‹x› (as in *brushes, dresses,* and *foxes*). These endings often sound like /z/ and /iz/, respectively, as in *girls* and *boxes*. Learning that these words are plurals will help the students remember to spell the /z/ sound correctly.

In the *Grammar 2 Student Book*, the students also learned the two ways of forming the plural of nouns that end with a ‹y›. If the letter immediately before the ‹y› is a vowel, then the plural is simply made in the usual way by adding ‹-s› (as in *days, boys,* and *monkeys*). However, if the letter immediately before the ⟨y⟩ is a consonant, then ⟨y⟩ is replaced by a "shy ⟨i⟩" before adding ⟨-es⟩ (as in *flies, babies,* and *puppies*). The students should already know that "shy ⟨i⟩" does not like to be at the end of a word and is often replaced by "toughy ⟨y⟩." This helps them understand that while we would be unlikely to find "shy ⟨i⟩" at the end of a word like *puppy*, we will find it in the plural, *puppies*, when "shy ⟨i⟩" is no longer at the end of the word.

The *Grammar 2 Student Book* also introduced some common irregular, or "tricky," plurals in the weekly spelling lists (e.g. *children* from *child, women* from *woman,* and *mice* from *mouse*). Tricky plurals can be formed by modifying the root word, altering its pronunciation, adding an unusual ending, or a combination of the three. Sometimes, the pronunciation of the root word alters even when the spelling does not; for instance, the letter ⟨i⟩ makes a long /ie/ sound in *child*, but a short /i/ sound in *children*. The *Grammar 3 Student Book* reviews regular plurals and introduces more irregular plurals, including nouns like *sheep, fish,* and *deer,* which are the same whether they are singular or plural.

Pronouns

Pronouns are the little words used to replace nouns. Without them, language would become boring and repetitive. They can be divided into personal pronouns (e.g. *I* and *me*), possessive pronouns (e.g. *mine*), relative pronouns (e.g. *who*), and reflexive pronouns (e.g. *myself*). Only personal pronouns were taught in the *Grammar 1* and *Grammar 2 Student Books*. Possessive pronouns are introduced in the *Grammar 3 Student Book*. The relative pronouns and reflexive pronouns can be taught when the students are older.

Personal Pronouns

In the *Grammar 1 Student Book*, the students were taught the eight personal pronouns: *I, you, he, she, it, we, you,* and *they*. In modern English, we use the same word, *you*, for both the second person singular pronoun and the second person plural pronoun, but this is not the case in many foreign languages. In order to make learning such languages easier later on, the *Grammar Student Books* introduce the students to the distinction between *you* used in the singular and *you* used in the plural.

In the *Grammar 3 Student Book*, the students learn how to identify the subject and the object of a sentence. They also learn that the personal pronouns can change, depending on whether they are the subject or the object of the sentence.

Subject Pronouns	I	you	he	she	it	we	you	they
Object Pronouns	me	you	him	her	it	us	you	them

The students practice using the subject pronouns whenever they conjugate verbs. They do the actions and say, for example, *I swim, you swim, he swims, she swims, it swims, we swim, you swim, they swim*. These same actions can also be used to review the object pronouns.

Singular Pronoun Actions:

I (me):	point to oneself
you (you):	point to someone else
he (him):	point to a boy
she (her):	point to a girl
it (it):	point to the floor

Plural Pronoun Actions:

we (us):	point in a circle including oneself and others
you (you):	point to two other people
they (them):	point to the next-door class

Color: The color for pronouns is pink.

Possessive Pronouns

There are eight possessive pronouns: *mine, yours, his, hers, its, ours, yours,* and *theirs.* These pronouns correspond to the personal pronouns: *I/me, you/you, he/him, she/her, it/it, we/us, you/you, they/them,* and the possessive adjectives: *my, your, his, her, its, our, your, their.* Possessive pronouns replace a noun and its possessive adjective, so that *my hat* becomes *mine,* and *their house* becomes *theirs.* These pronouns are possessive because they indicate who the noun (which they are also replacing) belongs to. Possessive pronouns can be practiced using the same color and actions as for the personal pronouns.

Verbs

A verb denotes what a person or thing does or is. It can describe an action, an event, a state, or a change. It is easiest for students to think of verbs as "doing words" at first. The infinitive form of a verb is made by putting the word *to* before the verb root, as in *to run, to hop, to sing,* and *to play.*

Action: The action for **verbs** in general is to clench fists and move arms backward and forward at one's sides, as if running.

Color: The color for all types of verb is red.

The students were introduced to verbs in the *Grammar 1 Student Book,* where they learned to conjugate regular verbs in the present, past, and future (because verbs in English are very complicated, only the simple tenses were introduced initially). Conjugating means choosing a particular verb and saying the pronouns in order with the correct form of the verb after each one. Conjugating verbs aloud with the pronoun actions is very good practice for students. It promotes a strong understanding of how verbs work, which helps them make sense of their own language and is invaluable when they come to learn foreign languages later on. Review the conjugations regularly, using the pronoun actions.

Past	*I jumped*	*you jumped*	*he jumped*	*she jumped*	*it jumped*
	we jumped	*you jumped*		*they jumped*	

Present	*I jump*	*you jump*	*he jumps*	*she jumps*	*it jumps*
	we jump	*you jump*		*they jump*	
Future	*I shall/will jump*	*you will jump*	*he will jump*	*she will jump*	*it will jump*
	we shall/will jump	*you will jump*		*they will jump*	

The students need to remember the following points:
- In the simple present tense, the verb changes after the first person singular pronouns: *he, she,* and *it*. For regular verbs, ‹-s› is added to the root (except when the word ends in ‹sh›, ‹ch›, ‹s›, ‹z›, or ‹x›, when ‹-es› is added). This is called the third person singular marker.
- The simple past tense of regular verbs is formed by adding the suffix ‹-ed› to the root. If the root ends in ‹e› (as in *bake*), the final ‹e› must be removed before ‹-ed› is added. The ‹-ed› can be pronounced in one of three ways: /t/ (as in *slipped*), /d/ (as in *smiled*), or /id/ (as in *waited*).
- With simple verbs, we add the auxiliary verbs *shall* or *will* to the verb root to denote the future. The auxiliary verb *will* can be used with all of the pronouns, but *shall* should only be used with *I* or *we* (the first person singular or the first person plural).

The students learned these regular conjugations in the *Grammar 1* and *Grammar 2 Student Books*, and continue to review them in the *Grammar 3 Student Book*. In the *Grammar 2 Student Book*, the students were also introduced to some of the most common irregular, or "tricky," verbs and their past forms: for example, *sat* (from *to sit*), and *ran* (from *to run*). In addition, they learned to conjugate and identify the irregular verb *to be* in both the present and past tenses. This is especially useful for those students who are not in the habit of using standard forms in their speech: students who say, for example, *we was* instead of *we were*. Chanting the conjugations regularly will help these students avoid making similar mistakes in their written work. The irregularity of the verb *to be* often makes it difficult for the students to identify it in sentences. It is important to overcome this problem, as the verb *to be* is used frequently. In the *Grammar 2 Student Book*, the students learned that every sentence must contain a verb and they were taught to identify sentences by looking for the verb. For this reason, it is crucial that the students are able to identify all verbs with confidence.

A familiarity with the verb *to be* will also help the students when they come to learn the continuous tenses, which are introduced in the *Grammar 3 Student Book*. The continuous tenses (e.g. *I am walking, I was walking, I shall be walking*) are formed by adding the present participle (e.g. *walking*) to the auxiliary verb *to be*. In order to form the continuous future, the students must first learn the future of the verb *to be*, which is introduced early on in the *Grammar 3 Student Book*. Once the students have learned how to form the continuous tenses, it is important to give them plenty of practice in identifying all of the verb tenses taught so far. In this way, they will be able to distinguish between the simple and continuous modes more easily and this in turn will help them understand how the different tenses are used.

For now, it is enough that the students understand that the simple present is used to describe an action that is repeated or usual (such as, *I swim in the pool every day*), and the present continuous is used to describe something that has started, is continuing, and has not stopped yet: either an action happening right now (e.g. *I am swimming in the pool*), or a longer action in progress, but one which is not necessarily happening at this moment (e.g. *I am learning to swim*). The simple past and simple future describe actions that have started and finished, or will start and finish, within a specific time (such as, *I swam in the pool today*, and *I shall swim in the pool later*), while the past and future continuous describe an on-going action.

There are other uses of these tenses, but they can be taught along with the perfect tenses when the students are older. For reference, the table below shows all three modes in past, present, and future.

	Past	Present	Future
Simple	*looked*	*look*	*will look*
Continuous	*was looking*	*is looking*	*will be looking*
Perfect	*had looked*	*have looked*	*will have looked*

In the *Grammar 2 Student Book*, the students were taught how to add the ‹-ing› suffix to verb roots. In the *Grammar 3 Student Book*, the students learn that this form of the verb is called the present participle. Later on, the students will learn that the present participle can be used to make the gerund form (the noun form) of a verb (e.g. *I like running*) and that it can be used as an adjective (e.g. *There was no running water*).

Technically there is no future tense in English since, unlike the past tense, the future is not formed by modifying the verb root itself. However, at this stage it is helpful for the students to think of verbs as taking place in the past, present, or future. The complexities of English grammar can be taught when the students are older.

Past Tense Action: The **past tense** action is pointing backward over one's shoulder with a thumb.

Present Tense Action: The **present tense** action is pointing toward the floor with the palm of the hand.

Future Action: The action for verbs that describe the **future** is pointing toward the front.

Adjectives

An adjective is a word that describes a noun or pronoun. It can be used either directly before the noun or pronoun, as in *the **big** dog*, or elsewhere in the sentence, as in *the dog was **big***. The students are encouraged to use adjectives imaginatively in their writing.

Action: The action for all types of **adjective**, including **possessive adjectives**, and **comparatives** and **superlatives**, is to touch the side of the temple with one's fist.

Color: The color for all types of adjective is blue.

Adjectives were introduced in the *Grammar 1 Student Book*, where the students learned how to use them before a noun. In the *Grammar 2 Student Book*, adjectives were reviewed, and the students practiced identifying them wherever they were placed in the sentence. In the *Grammar 3 Student Book*, the students learn that adjectives can be formed by adding certain suffixes to other words: for example, by adding the suffix ‹-y› to a noun (e.g. *windy, salty, stormy*), or by adding the suffixes ‹-less› and ‹-able› to words (e.g. *flawless, enjoyable*).

In the *Grammar 3 Student Book*, the students also learn that sometimes nouns can act as adjectives. For example, in *apple pie*, the first noun, *apple*, is describing the main noun, *pie*.

Possessive Adjectives

The students' understanding of adjectives was extended in the *Grammar 2 Student Book* to include the eight possessive adjectives: *my, your, his, her, its, our, your,* and *their*. These correspond to the personal pronouns: *I/me, you/you, he/him, she/her, it/it, we/us, you/you, they/them*, and the possessive pronouns: *mine, yours, his, hers, its, ours, yours, theirs*. A possessive adjective replaces one noun and describes another, by saying whose it is. For example, in the sentence *Lucy fed her cat*, the possessive adjective *her* is used in place of *Lucy's* and describes *cat*, by saying whose cat it is. (As the possessive adjectives also function as pronouns, they are sometimes known as the "weak" set of possessive pronouns. However, to avoid any confusion with the "strong" set of possessive pronouns, like *mine*, the *Grammar Student and Teacher's Books* do not use this terminology.)

Comparatives and Superlatives

The adjectives introduced in the *Grammar 1 Student Book* are called positive adjectives; they describe a noun or a pronoun without comparing it to anything else (as in *the girl is **young***). In the *Grammar 2 Student Book*, comparative and superlative adjectives were introduced. These adjectives describe a noun or a pronoun by comparing it to other items. A comparative is used when comparing a noun to one or more other items (as in *this boy is **younger** than Jim and Ted*). A superlative is used when comparing a noun to the other items in a group to which that noun also belongs (as in *he is the **youngest** boy on the team*). Short positive adjectives usually form their comparatives and superlatives with the suffixes ‹-er› and ‹-est›: for example, *hard, harder, hardest*. With longer adjectives, we often use the words *more* and *most*: for example, *difficult, more difficult, most difficult*. It is important that the students learn to add the ‹-er› and ‹-est› suffixes correctly (see the rules for adding suffixes on page 25). With the students, practice saying an adjective followed by its comparative and superlative: for example, *clean, cleaner, cleanest*. Ask the students which spelling they would use in each case.

Adverbs

An adverb is similar to an adjective, in that they are both describing words. However, an adverb describes a verb rather than a noun. Usually, adverbs describe how,

Action: The action for an **adverb** is to bang one fist on top of the other.
Color: The color for adverbs is orange.

where, when, or how often something happens. Adverbs can also be used to modify adjectives or other adverbs, but the students do not need to know that at this stage.

    The students were introduced to adverbs in the *Grammar 1 Student Book*. Initially, they were taught to think of an adverb as a word often ending with the suffix ‹-ly›. In the *Grammar 2 Student Book,* adverbs were reviewed and the students were encouraged to identify less obvious adverbs by looking at the verb and deciding which word describes it. For example, in the sentence, *We arrived late last night*, the adverb *late* tells us something about the past tense verb *arrived*. Point out examples of adverbs in text whenever possible to help the students develop this understanding. In the *Grammar 3 Student Book*, the students learn that adjectives can sometimes be turned into adverbs by adding the suffix ‹-ly›, as in *quickly, slowly,* and *softly*.

Prepositions

A preposition is a word that relates one noun or pronoun to another. (Later, when the students learn about subjects and objects, they will learn that a preposition relates the subject of a sentence to the object.) In the sentence, *He climbed over the gate*, for example, the preposition *over* relates the subject, *he*, to the object, *gate*. The "pre-" of preposition means *before* and "position" means *place*, so together preposition means *placed before*, because it is placed before a noun or pronoun. A preposition is also placed before any describing words that may already come before the noun or pronoun (words such as adjectives, possessive adjectives, or the articles *a, an,* and *the*), as in the phrases **after** *a long pause,* **by** *her favorite author,* **in** *my purse,* **under** *the bridge*.

> Action: The action for **prepositions** is to point from one noun to another.
> Color: The color for prepositions is green.

Prepositions, as introduced in the *Grammar 2 Student Book*, often describe where something is or what it is moving toward. Practice prepositions by calling out examples and asking for nouns to go with them. For example, for *in*, the students might suggest *the box* or *the classroom*, and for *under* they might suggest *the mat* or *the table*. Many common prepositions are short words like *at, by, for, of, in, on, to,* and *up*. Other common examples include: *above, after, around, behind, beside, between, down, from, into, past, through, toward, under,* and *with*. However, many of these words can also function as adverbs if they do not come before a noun or pronoun. For example, in the sentence, *I fell down*, the word *down* is an adverb that describes *fell*, whereas in *I fell down the stairs*, the word *down* is a preposition that relates *I* to *stairs*.

Conjunctions

A conjunction is a word used to join parts of a sentence that usually, but not always, contain their own verbs. The *Grammar 2 Student Book* introduced conjunctions, focusing on six of the most useful ones: *and,*

> Action: The action for **conjunctions** is to hold one's hands apart with palms facing up. Move both hands so one is on top of the other.
> Color: The color for conjunctions is purple.

but, because, or, so, and *while*. Other common conjunctions include: *although, if, now, once, since, unless, until, when,* and *whether*. Conjunctions allow the students to write longer, less repetitive sentences. Instead of writing, for example, *I eat burgers. I eat fries. I like the taste*, the students could use the conjunctions *and* and *because* to write: *I eat burgers and fries because I like the taste*. Where the shorter sentences were stilted and repetitive, the new one is flowing and concise. The ability to vary the length of their sentences will greatly improve the quality of the students' writing. Display a list of common conjunctions in the classroom to encourage the students to use alternatives to *and*.

Definite and Indefinite Articles: the, a, an

The words *a, an,* and *the* are known as articles. *A* and *an* are used before singular nouns and are called the indefinite articles, as in *a man* and *an egg. The* is used before singular and plural nouns and is called the definite article, as in *the dog* and *the boys*. The articles are a special sort of adjective, although the term *determiner* is often used as well. Determiners are words used in front of nouns to show, or determine, which things or people are being referred to.

In the *Grammar 1 Student Book*, the students learned when to use *an* instead of *a*. They were taught to choose the correct article by looking at the noun that follows it. When the noun begins with a vowel sound, the correct article is *an*, as in *an ant, an eagle, an igloo, an octopus, an umpire*. Otherwise, the correct article is *a*. Note that it is the first sound that is important, not necessarily the first letter. If, for example, a word starts with a silent consonant and the first sound is actually a vowel, the correct article is *an*, as in *an hour*. If, on the other hand, the word starts with the long vowel /ue/, pronounced /y-oo/, then the correct article is *a*, as in *a unicorn*.

Sentences and Phrases

It is difficult to define a sentence in a way that can be readily understood by young students. However, there are some simple rules that they can learn easily. In the *Grammar 1 Student Book,* the students learned that a sentence must start with a capital letter, end with a period, and make sense. In the *Grammar 2 Student Book* this definition was refined, and the students learned that a sentence must always have a verb and must end with a period, question mark, or exclamation mark. The definition is further refined in the *Grammar 3 Student Book*, when the students learn that a sentence must also have a subject, and may have an object too. The subject is the noun or pronoun that "does" the verb action, and the object is the noun or pronoun that "receives" the verb action. So in a sentence like *Sam hit the ball, Sam* is the subject and the *ball* is the object. Whereas, in *The ball hit Sam*, the *ball* is the subject and *Sam* is the object.

In the *Grammar 3 Student Book*, phrases are introduced with this simple working definition: when a group of words makes sense but has no verb, it is called a phrase. At this stage, it is enough that the students are able to distinguish between a sentence and a phrase, and expand a phrase into a complete sentence.

Paragraphs

In the *Grammar 3 Student Book,* the students begin to learn about paragraphs. Paragraphs are used to organize information in a piece of writing so that it is easy to read and understand. Instead of one large block of text, writing is broken down into smaller groups of sentences called paragraphs. Each paragraph starts on a new line and is made up of sentences that describe one idea or topic. By putting paragraphs in a particular order, a piece of writing can move from one idea to another in a way that makes sense.

The students are encouraged to think about what they want to say and organize their thoughts before they start writing. They learn how to break down the topic they want to write about into "subtopics" and place their different ideas under "subheadings." This helps them to make their writing flow and be more interesting. The students should be encouraged to write in paragraphs from now on.

Punctuation

The *Grammar Student Books* emphasize the importance of punctuation. The teaching aims to help the students understand that their writing will be easier to read if it is accurately punctuated. In the *Grammar 2 Student Book*, the students reviewed periods, question marks, and speech marks (also known as quotation marks), and were introduced to exclamation marks, commas, and apostrophes.

In the *Grammar 3 Student Book*, the focus is on using the correct punctuation when writing direct speech. In direct speech, the words are written exactly as they are said: for example, *"I'm tired," said Tim.* (This is different from reported speech: for example, *Tim said he was tired.*) The students also review speech marks, periods, commas, and contractions, and learn how to use question marks and exclamation marks in direct speech.

Question Marks ‹?›

The students need to understand what a question is and how to form a question mark correctly. If a sentence is worded in such a way that it expects an answer, then it is a question and needs a question mark instead of a period. The students have learned that common questions often start with one of the ‹wh› words (*what, why, when, where, who, which, whose*). If the question is being written as direct speech, the question mark is kept at the end and not replaced with a comma.

Exclamation Marks ‹!›

An exclamation mark (also known as an exclamation point) is used at the end of a sentence, instead of a period, to show that the speaker or writer feels strongly about something. When someone exclaims, they cry out suddenly, especially in anger, surprise, or pain. What they say is called an exclamation. If the exclamation is being written as direct speech, the exclamation mark is kept at the end and not replaced with a comma.

Commas ‹,›

Sometimes it is necessary to indicate a short pause in the middle of a sentence, where it would be wrong to use a period. This helps the reader separate one idea from another. For this sort of pause we use a comma. The students will be used to being told to pause when they see a comma in their reading. However, learning when to use commas in writing is more difficult. The *Grammar 2 Student Book* introduced two of the most straightforward ways commas are used:

1. We use commas to separate items in a list of more than two items: *red, white, and blue,* or *Grandma, Grandpa, Aunt, and Uncle.* Note that before the last item in a list, the comma is followed by the word *and* or *or.*

2. We also use commas in sentences that include direct speech. Here, the comma indicates a pause between the words spoken and the rest of the sentence. If the speech comes before the rest of the sentence, the comma belongs after the last word spoken but inside the speech marks: *"I am hungry," complained Matt.* (If the words spoken are a question or an exclamation, then a question mark or exclamation mark is used instead of a comma in the same position.) If the speech comes after the rest of the sentence, the comma belongs after the last word that is not spoken but before the speech marks: *Matt complained, "I am hungry."*

Apostrophes ‹'›

The *Grammar 2 Student Book* introduced both of the main ways that an apostrophe is used. Apostrophes are very often incorrectly used. There are clear rules for using apostrophes and it is important to teach them early on before any students develop bad habits in their writing.

• An apostrophe followed by the letter ‹s› is used after a noun to indicate possession, as in *Ben's new toy* or *the girl's father.* The apostrophe is needed to show that the ‹s› is not being used to make a plural. Understanding this distinction will help the students use apostrophe ‹s› correctly. Encourage the students to think about the meaning of what they write and decide whether each ‹s› is being used to make a plural or the possessive case. Later on, they will learn how to use apostrophe ‹s› with plurals that end in ‹s› (e.g. *the boys' room*) and names that end in ‹es› (e.g. *James' cat*).

   Although the possessive adjectives (e.g. *my, your, his*) indicate possession, there is no risk of confusion with the plural, so they do not need an apostrophe. However, it is important to help the students avoid the common mistake of writing the possessive adjective *its* as *it's.*

• An apostrophe is also used to show that a letter (or more than one letter) is missing. Sometimes, we shorten a pair of words by joining them together and leaving out some of their letters. We use an apostrophe to show where the missing letter (or letters) used to be. This is called a contraction. There are many common contractions, such as *I'm* (I am), *didn't* (did not), and *you'll* (you will).

   Encourage the students to listen to each contraction and identify which sound or sounds are missing. This will help them to leave out the appropriate letters and put the apostrophe in the right place, thereby avoiding some common mistakes. In *haven't,* for example, the /o/ of *not* is missing, so the apostrophe goes between ‹n› and ‹t›, to show where ‹o› used to be. It does not go between ‹e› and ‹n›, as in "have'nt." When *it is* is contracted to *it's*, as in *it's late*, an apostrophe is needed to show that the second ‹i› is missing. The students need to think about the meaning of what they are writing, so as to avoid confusion with the possessive adjective *its*. It is important that the students learn how to spell and punctuate contractions correctly. However, they should only use contractions when writing direct speech or informal notes. Contractions are not traditionally used in formal writing.

Parsing: identifying parts of speech in sentences

Parsing means identifying the function, or part of speech, of each word in a sentence. The students must look at each word in context to decide what part of speech it is. This skill is worth promoting, as it reinforces the grammar teaching and helps the students to develop an analytical understanding of how our language works. Many words can function as more than one part of speech. For example, the word *light* can be a noun (*the light*), a verb (*to light*), or an adjective (*a light color*). It is only by analyzing a word's use within a sentence that its function can be identified.

Begin by writing extremely simple sentences on the board. A good example is: *I pat the dog*. This can be parsed as: pronoun, verb, (article,) noun. Ask the students to identify the parts of speech they know. They enjoy taking turns to underline the parts of speech in the appropriate colors. Gradually, when most of the students have mastered this, move on to more complicated sentences that use more parts of speech: for example, *She cheerfully wrote a long letter to her friend*. This can be parsed as: pronoun, adverb, verb (the infinitive of which is *to write*), (article,) adjective, noun, preposition, possessive adjective, noun. Remind the students that every sentence must contain at least one verb. They should begin parsing a sentence by identifying the verb or verbs, and should supply each verb in the infinitive form. If there is time, the students should identify as many of the other parts of speech as possible, underlining them in the appropriate colors (as shown in the parsing color key below).

Nouns	**Verbs**	Pronouns	**Adjectives**	Adverbs	**Prepositions**	**Conjunctions**
(Black)	(Red)	(Pink)	(Blue)	(Orange)	(Green)	(Purple)

In the *Grammar 3 Student Book*, the regular parsing practice in the spelling lessons will help the students become quick and competent at this task.

Alphabetical Order, Dictionary, and Thesaurus Work

Many reference materials, including dictionaries, thesauruses, and encyclopedias, organize their material alphabetically. The more familiar the students are with the order of the alphabet, the better they will be at using these resources independently.

In the *Grammar 1 Student Book*, the students were introduced to alphabetical order and to using a dictionary. To help them find words, the students were encouraged to think of the dictionary as being divided into four approximately equal parts, as shown on the following page.

1. **A a B b C c D d E e**
2. **F f G g H h I i J j K k L l M m**
3. **N n O o P p Q q R r S s**
4. **T t U u V v W w X x Y y Z z**

Knowing these letter groups saves the students time when using the dictionary. Before looking up a word, they decide which group its initial letter falls into, and then narrow their search to that section of the dictionary. For the word *pony*, for example, the first letter is ‹p›, which is in the third group, so the students would turn to the third quarter of the dictionary. For easy reference there is a copy of the alphabet, divided up into the four color-coded groups, on the first page of the *Grammar 3 Student Book*.

The *Grammar 2 Student Book* improved the students' dictionary skills by teaching them to look beyond the initial letter of each word. The students practiced putting into alphabetical order words that share the first two letters: for example, *sheep, shoe, ship,* and then words that share the first three letters: for example, *penny, pencil, penguin*. This skill is reinforced in the *Grammar 3 Student Book*, where a common activity in the spelling lessons involves putting the words from the spelling list into alphabetical order.

Most students can become quite proficient at using a dictionary designed for schools. When they finish a piece of writing, the students should proofread their work, identify any words that look incorrectly spelled, and look them up in the dictionary. The students should also be encouraged to use the dictionary to look up meanings. In the *Grammar 2 Student Book,* for example, the students practice using a dictionary to help them distinguish between homophones (such as *hear* and *here,* and *where* and *wear*). Regular activities in the spelling lessons of the *Grammar 3 Student Book* require the students to look up words for spelling and meaning. This helps them understand how useful dictionaries can be and aims to develop the skills they need to become regular and proficient dictionary users. The students were also introduced to thesauruses in the *Grammar 2 Student Book*. (These books list words by meaning, collating words with similar meanings to one another.) The students should be encouraged to make their work more interesting by finding alternatives to words that are commonly overused, such as *nice*.

It can be helpful to give each student a "Spelling Word Book" for listing words with a particular spelling pattern and keeping a note of any homophones or unusual words they come across. These books can then be used to help the students in their independent writing. The following extension ideas are also useful for improving alphabet and dictionary skills, or for those students who finish their work ahead of time.

- The students take the words from one page of their Spelling Word Book and rewrite them in alphabetical order.
- The students use the dictionary to choose the correct spelling of a word. For this activity, write out a word three or four times on the board. Spell it slightly differently each time, but ensure that one of the spellings is correct. It is a good idea to choose a word that contains a sound with alternative spellings: for example, *disturb*, which contains the /er/ sound. This word could be spelled *disterb, distirb,* or *disturb*. The students write the correct spelling in their Spelling Word Book.
- In pairs, the students race one another to find a given word in the dictionary.

Teaching Ideas for Spelling

Most students need to be taught to spell correctly. In the *Grammar Student Books*, spelling is the main focus for one lesson each week. The spelling activities in the *Grammar 3 Student Book* are designed to consolidate the students' existing knowledge, introduce new spelling patterns, and review alternative spellings of the vowel sounds.

The students first learned to spell by listening for the sounds in a word and writing the letters that represent those sounds, and by systematically learning the spellings of key irregular, or "tricky," words. After completing the *Phonics* and *Grammar 1 Student Books*, most students have a reading age of at least seven years and are starting to spell with far greater accuracy. As research has shown, students with a reading age of seven years or more are able to use analogy in their reasoning. This is a useful strategy for spelling. Students who want to write *should*, for example, might notice that the end of this word sounds very like that of a word they already know, such as *would*. They could then use the spelling of *would* to write *should*, replacing the ‹w› with ‹sh›. If the students are unsure of a spelling, they may be able to find it by writing the word in several ways (e.g. *should* and "shood"), and choosing the version that looks correct. If they have already encountered the word several times in their reading, they will probably be able to choose the right spelling. By introducing groups of spelling words that each feature a particular spelling pattern, the *Grammar Student Books* encourage the students to think analogically.

The *Grammar 3 Student Book* reviews previously taught alternative spellings for the vowel sounds alongside introducing new alternative spelling patterns. This helps the students to consolidate and extend their learning. By this stage, the students need to learn the main ways of spelling each of the vowel sounds and which words take which spelling. The *Grammar 3 Student Book* covers the following spelling features, which are outlined in greater detail below.

1. Vowel Digraphs
2. Alternative Letter Sound Spellings
3. New Spelling Patterns
4. Silent Letters
5. Syllables
6. Identifying the Short Vowels
7. Spelling Rules

1. Vowel Digraphs

The vowel digraphs were introduced in *Jolly Phonics* and the *Grammar 1 Student Book*. The focus in the *Grammar 2* and *Grammar 3 Student Books* is on consolidating this learning. *Vowel digraph* is the term for two letters that make a single vowel sound. At least one of these letters is always a vowel. Often, the two letters are placed next to each other in a word: for example, the ‹ay› in *hay* and the ‹ew› in *few*. Two vowel letters are usually needed to make a long vowel sound. The long vowel sounds are the same as the names of the vowel letters: /ai/, /ee/, /ie/, /oa/, /ue/. Generally, the sound

made by the digraph is that of the first vowel's name. Hence the well-known rule of thumb: "When two vowels go walking, the first does the talking."

Sometimes, the long vowel sound is made by two vowels separated by one or more consonants. In monosyllabic words, the second vowel is usually an ‹e›, known as a "magic ‹e›" because it modifies the sound of the first vowel letter. Digraphs with a magic ‹e› can be thought of as "hop-over ‹e›" digraphs: ‹a_e›, ‹e_e›, ‹i_e›, ‹o_e›, and ‹u_e›. Once again, the sound they make is that of the first vowel's name; the "magic ‹e›" is silent. Students like to show with their hands how the "magic" from the ‹e› hops over the preceding consonant and changes the short vowel sound to a long one.

The hop-over ‹e› digraphs are an alternative way of making the long vowel sounds, and are found in such words as *bake, these, fine, hope,* and *cube.* The students need to be shown many examples of hop-over ‹e› digraphs. It is possible to illustrate the function of the magic ‹e› in such words by using a piece of paper to cover the ‹e›, and reading the word first with the magic ‹e›, and then without it. For example, *pipe* becomes *pip* without the magic ‹e›; *hate* becomes *hat; hope* becomes *hop;* and *late* becomes *lat.* The students may like to do this themselves. It does not matter if, as in the *late/lat* example, they find themselves producing nonsense words. The exercise will still help them to understand the spelling rule. When looking at text on the board or in big books, the students can be encouraged to look for and identify words with a magic ‹e›.

Although hop-over ‹e› words are generally quite common, there are only a few words with the ‹e_e› spelling pattern. Examples include: *these, scheme,* and *complete.* Words with an ‹e_e› spelling are not only rather rare, but often quite advanced. For this reason, the ‹e_e› spelling is not given quite as much emphasis as the other long vowel spellings, and is not made the focus of a whole lesson until the *Grammar 3 Student Book.*

2. Alternative Letter Sound Spellings

Students who have learned to read with *Jolly Phonics* are used to spelling new words by listening for the sounds and writing the letters that represent those sounds. This skill enables the students to spell accurately the many regular words that do not contain sounds with more than one spelling, words like *hot, plan, brush, drench,* and *sting.* However, words like *train, play,* and *make* present a problem for spelling. All three words feature the same vowel sound: /ai/, but in each case it is spelled differently. The table opposite shows the first spelling taught for each sound and the main alternatives introduced.

The alternative spellings of vowel sounds were introduced and then reviewed in the *Grammar 1* and *Grammar 2 Student Books,* and

First spelling taught	Alternative spellings for sound	Examples of all spellings in words
‹ai›	‹ay›, ‹a_e›	*rain, day, came*
‹ee›	‹ea›, ‹e_e›	*street, dream, these*
‹ie›	‹y›, ‹i_e›, ‹igh›	*pie, by, time, light*
‹oa›	‹ow›, ‹o_e›	*boat, snow, home*
‹ue›	‹ew›, ‹u_e›	*cue, few, cube*
‹er›	‹ir›, ‹ur›	*her, first, turn*
‹oi›	‹oy›	*boil, toy*
‹ou›	‹ow›	*out, cow*
‹or›	‹al›, ‹au›, ‹aw›	*for, sauce, talk, saw*
‹air›	‹are›, ‹ear›	*hair, care, bear*
‹k›	‹ck›	*park, cricket*
‹f›	‹ph›	*fin, photo*
‹s›	"soft ‹c›"	*sit, cycle*
‹j›	"soft ‹g›"	*jam, gymnast*
‹w›	‹wh›	*wig, whale*

should be familiar to the students. The alternative vowel spellings are what makes English spelling difficult and it is very important to consolidate this teaching. This can be achieved by reviewing the spelling patterns regularly with flash cards, and by asking the students to list the alternative spellings for a particular sound. The students should be able to do this automatically and apply their knowledge when writing unfamiliar words. For example, with a word like *frame*, they should be able to write "fraim, fraym, frame" on a scrap of paper, before deciding which version looks correct.

3. New Spelling Patterns

The *Grammar 2* and *Grammar 3 Student Books* introduce many of the less common spellings of familiar sounds. The tables opposite show the spellings first taught, and the new spelling patterns introduced.

The students need to memorize which words use each of these new spelling patterns. It is helpful to make up silly sentences for each spelling, using as many of the words as possible. For example, for the ‹ie› spelling of the /ee/ sound, the students could chant the following: *I believe my niece was the chief thief who came to grief over the piece of shield she hid in the field.*

In the *Grammar 2* and *Grammar 3 Student Books*, the students learned some new sounds that were not included in the *Phonics* and *Grammar 1 Student Books*. For example, the /ear/ sound was introduced initially in the *Grammar 2 Student Book* as ‹ear› as in *hear* and *earrings*. In the *Grammar 3 Student Book*, the students learn the alternative spellings, ‹eer› and ‹ere›, as in *deer* and *cheer*, and *here* and *mere*. Similarly, the /air/ sound was introduced initially as ‹air›, ‹are›, and ‹ear›, as in *hair*, *care*, and *bear*. The *Grammar 3 Student Book* teaches the ‹ere› spelling, as in *there*, *ere*, and *where*. The students' knowledge of ‹ure› is also reviewed and extended in the *Grammar 3 Student Book*. The students review the /cher/ sound made by ‹ture› in a word like *picture*, and learn that ‹ure› often

Spellings taught in the *Grammar 2 Student Book*		
First spelling taught for sound(s)	New spelling(s) for sound(s)	Examples of new spellings in words
‹ai›	‹ei›, ‹eigh›	*veil, eighteen*
cher*	‹ture›	*capture, nature*
‹e›	‹ea›	*breakfast, ready*
‹ee›	‹ey›, ‹ie›	*chimney, field*
‹k›	‹ch›	*chemist, chord*
eer*	‹ear›	*year, earrings*
‹or›	‹ore›	*more, snore, wore*
‹sh› / zh*	‹si›	*tension, vision*
‹sh›*	‹ti›	*fiction, station*
‹u›	‹o›, ‹ou›	*month, young*
ool*	‹-le›	*handle, little*
‹wo›	‹wa›	*swan, was, wasp*

Spellings taught in the *Grammar 3 Student Book*		
First spelling taught for sound(s)	New spelling(s) for sound(s)	Examples of new spellings in words
‹ai›	‹a›	*able, taste, haste*
‹air›, ‹are›, ‹ear›	‹ere›	*where, there*
‹ch›	‹tch›	*match, itch, fetch*
‹ear›*	‹eer›, ‹ere›	*cheer, deer, here*
‹ee›	‹e›, ‹e_e›	*athlete, secret*
‹f›	‹gh›	*enough, cough*
‹i›	‹y›	*myth, pyramid*
‹ie›	‹i›	*child, wild*
‹j›	‹dge›	*edge, bridge, judge*
‹n›	‹gn›	*gnome, resign*
‹ng›	‹n›	*trunk, finger*
‹oa›	‹o›	*only, ogre, ago*
‹o› (after ‹qu›)	‹a› (after ‹qu›)	*squad, quantity*
‹ue›	‹u›	*menu, emu*
‹z›	‹s›, ‹se›, ‹ze›	*easy, pause, bronze*

* As the relevant lesson plans explain, this is only an approximation of the sound made by the new spelling.

follows ‹s› to make words like *pleasure* and *treasure*, where the ‹s› makes a /zh/ sound. The ‹ure› spelling pattern can also follow other letters to make words like *figure*, *failure*, and *conjure*.

4. Silent Letters

A number of English words contain letters that are not pronounced at all. These are known as silent letters. Some silent letters, such as the ‹k› in *knee*, show us how the word was pronounced in the past. Other silent letters, like the ‹h› in *rhyme*, indicate the word's foreign origins. The *Grammar Student Books* introduce the following silent letters:

- silent ‹b›, as in *lamb*
- silent ‹c›, as in *scissors*
- silent ‹h›, as in *rhubarb*
- silent ‹k›, as in *knife*
- silent ‹w›, as in *wrong*
- silent ‹g›, as in *gnome*.

The *Grammar 2 Student Book* introduced the first five silent letters. The *Grammar 3 Student Book* introduces silent ‹g› as part of the spelling pattern ‹gn›, which says the /n/ sound. Practicing with the "say it as it sounds" technique helps students remember these spellings. For the word *lamb*, for example, say the word to the class, pronouncing it correctly as /lam/. The students respond by saying /lamb/, emphasizing the /b/, which would normally be silent.

5. Syllables

An understanding of syllables will help to improve the students' spelling. A number of spelling rules depend on the students' ability to identify the number of syllables in a given word. Knowing about syllables will also help the students later on when they begin to learn about where the stress is placed in words. Although the rules of English sometimes let us down, they are worth acquiring. The more the students know, the more skillful they become, and the better equipped they are to deal with any irregularities.

In the *Grammar 2 Student Book* the students were encouraged to count the syllables in words using "chin bumps." Chin bumps are a fun, multisensory way of teaching syllables. The students place one hand under their chin (with the hand flattened as though they are about to pat something). Then they slowly say a word, and count the number of times they feel their chin go down and bump on their hand. For *cat*, for example, they will feel one bump, which means it has one syllable. *Table* has two bumps, so two syllables; *any* has two bumps and two syllables; *screeched* has one bump and one syllable; and *idea* has three bumps and three syllables.

In the *Grammar 3 Student Book*, the teaching of syllables is extended and refined. The students learn that syllables are units of sound organized around the vowel sounds. If a word has three vowel sounds, for example, it will have three syllables. (Words with three or more syllables are referred to as multisyllabic, or polysyllabic.) If a word only has one vowel sound, and therefore one syllable, it is called a monosyllabic word.

The students are given regular practice identifying the syllables in words. They will find doing this aurally (using chin bumps or by clapping the syllables) quite easy with practice. The students are also encouraged to identify syllables on paper, by identifying the letters making the vowel sounds and then drawing a line between the syllables. There are some simple rules the students can learn to help them split words with double consonants, or with ‹ck› and ‹le› spellings (see page 55). Exactly how a word is split into syllables often depends on whether the syllable is "open" or "closed." Open syllables are syllables ending in a long vowel sound, and closed syllables are syllables with a short vowel that end in a consonant. The type of syllable is not always easy to determine, as many long vowels become swallowed and are pronounced as schwas in English. The guidance given in the lesson plans aims to follow these rules, but in practice there is no definitive way to split the syllables and different dictionaries will often do it in different ways. For now, the focus should be on improving the students' ability to identify the vowel sounds in a word and hear how many syllables there are.

6. Identifying the Short Vowels

One of the most reliable spelling rules in English is the consonant doubling rule. Consonant doubling is governed by the short vowels, so the students need to be able to identify short vowel sounds confidently. In the *Grammar 1* and *Grammar 2 Student Books*, a puppet was used to encourage the students to listen for the short vowels.

- For /a/, put the puppet at the side of the box.
- For /e/, make the puppet wobble on the edge of the box.
- For /i/, put the puppet in the box.
- For /o/, put the puppet on the box.
- For /u/, put the puppet under the box.

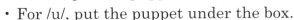

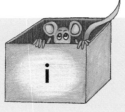

The students pretended that their fist was the box and their hand was the puppet.

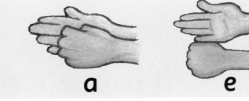

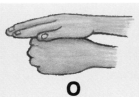
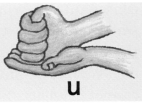

Initially, the students were encouraged to do the appropriate action when the short vowel sounds were called out. Then, they learned to do the actions when they heard short words with a short vowel sound (e.g. *pot, hat, bun, dig, red*). Once the students had learned to distinguish between short vowels and long vowels (and the other vowel sounds) they were able to do the appropriate short vowel action when short words with a variety of vowel sounds were called out. For those that did not have a short vowel sound, the students kept their hands still.

In the *Grammar 3 Student Book*, the students are encouraged to review the short vowel sounds regularly using the vowel hand. They hold up one hand so their palm is facing them; then, using the index finger of the other hand, they point to the tip of each finger, saying the vowel sounds in turn. First they point to the tip of the thumb for /a/, then to the first finger for /e/, and so on. Then, as they review the long vowel sounds, they can point to the base of each finger as they say /ai/, /ee/, /ie/, /oa/, and /ue/. Activities like these help to keep the students "tuned in" to identifying the sounds in words and, in turn, help to prepare them for the consonant doubling rules.

7. Spelling Rules

An ability to identify syllables and short vowels will help the students apply the following rules for consonant doubling and adding suffixes.

Spelling Rules for Consonant Doubling

a. In a monosyllabic word with a short vowel sound, ending in ‹f›, ‹l›, ‹s›, or ‹z›, the final consonant letter is doubled, as in the words *cliff, bell, miss,* and *buzz.* (The only exceptions to this rule include the tricky two-letter words: *as, if, is, of,* and *us.*)

b. In a monosyllabic word with a short vowel sound, if the last consonant sound is /k/, this is spelled ‹ck›, as in the words: *back, neck, lick, clock,* and *duck.*

c. If there is only one consonant after a short, stressed vowel sound, this consonant is doubled before any suffix starting with a vowel is added. For example, when the suffixes ‹-ed›, ‹-er›, ‹-est›, ‹-ing›, ‹-y›, and ‹-able› are added to the words *hop, wet, big, clap, fun,* and *hug,* the final consonants are doubled so that we get *hopped, wetter, biggest, clapping, funny,* and *huggable.* Note that when ‹y› is a suffix, it counts as a vowel because it has a vowel sound. (This rule does not apply to those words where the final consonant is ‹x›, because ‹x› is really the two consonant sounds /k/ and /s/. This means that ‹x› is never doubled, even in words like *faxed, boxing,* and *mixer.*) It can help if the students think of the two consonants as forming a "wall." If there were only one consonant, the wall would not be thick enough to prevent "magic" hopping over from the vowel in the suffix and changing the short vowel sound to a long one. With two consonants, the wall becomes so thick that the "magic" cannot get over. (See: Spelling Rules for Adding Suffixes, rule c.)

d. When a word ends with the letters ‹le› and the preceding syllable contains a short, stressed vowel sound, there must be two consonants between the short vowel and the ‹-le›. This means that the consonant before the ‹-le› is doubled in words like *paddle, kettle, nibble, topple,* and *snuggle.* No doubling is necessary in words like *handle, twinkle,* and *jungle* because they already have two consonants between the short vowel and the ‹le›.

Spelling Rules for Adding Suffixes

a. If the root word ends with a consonant that is not immediately preceded by a short vowel sound, simply add the suffix. So, *walk* + ‹-ed› = *walked, quick* + ‹-est› = *quickest, look* + ‹-ing› = *looking*, and *avoid* + ‹-able› = *avoidable*.

b. If the root word ends with the letter ‹e› and the suffix starts with a vowel, remove the ‹e› before adding the suffix. So, *love* + ‹-ed› = *loved, brave* + ‹-er› = *braver, like* + ‹-ing› = *liking*, and *value* + ‹-able› = *valuable*, but *care* + ‹-less› = *careless*.

    The main exception to this rule is when the suffix ‹-ing› is added to a root word that has an ‹i› before the ‹e›, as in *tie*. To avoid having two ‹i›s next to each other (e.g. "tiing"), both the ‹i› and the ‹e› are replaced with a ‹y›. So *tie* + ‹-ing› = *tying* and *lie* + ‹-ing› = *lying*, even though these same words become *tied* and *lied* when adding ‹-ed›. Another exception is when the ‹e› is part of the soft ‹c› or soft ‹g› spelling and the suffix ‹-able› is added. In this instance, the ‹e› is kept so that ‹c› is pronounced /s/ and ‹g› is pronounced /j/, as in *noticeable* and *changeable*. (Some words can be spelled either with or without the ‹e›, so both *lovable* and *loveable* are correct; however, in these cases it is better for the students to be consistent and drop the ‹e› in their writing.)

c. If the root word ends with a consonant that is immediately preceded by a short, stressed vowel sound and the suffix begins with a vowel, double the final consonant before adding the suffix. So, *stop* + ‹-ed› = *stopped, sad* + ‹-er› = *sadder, run* + ‹-ing› = *running*, and *control* + ‹-able› = *controllable*, but *sad* + ‹-ness› = *sadness*. Remind the students that two consonants are needed to make a "wall," to prevent "magic" from the vowel in the suffix from jumping over to change the short vowel sound. (See: Spelling Rules for Consonant Doubling, rule c.)

d. If the root word ends with the letter ‹y›, which is immediately preceded by a consonant, replace the ‹y› with an ‹i› before adding the suffix. So, *hurry* + ‹-ed› = *hurried, dirty* + ‹-est› = *dirtiest, beauty* + ‹-ful› = *beautiful, vary* + ‹-able› = *variable*, and *pity* + ‹-ful› = *pitiful*. However, if the suffix starts with the letter ‹i›, the rule does not apply, so *worry* + ‹-ing› = *worrying*.

    The letter ‹y› is unique in being able to function as either a vowel or a consonant. As a vowel, ‹y› replaces ‹i›. In the *Phonics Student Books*, the students learned that "shy ‹i›" does not like to go at the end of a word, so "toughy ‹y›" takes its place. As the last syllable of a multisyllabic word, the sound ‹y› makes is somewhere between the short /i/ in *tin* and the long /ee/ in *bee*. (This is also true of the rare instances when the letter ‹i› is the final syllable of a polysyllabic word, as in *taxi*.) Despite this confusing pronunciation, it is important for the students to think of ‹y› as replacing "shy ‹i›." This will help them remember that the ‹i› returns when such words are extended (except in words like *worrying*, where it would look odd to have two ‹i›s next to each other).

In the *Grammar Student Books*, suffixes and prefixes are introduced with prefix and suffix fish. Prefixes are shown on the fish's head, the root (or *base*) word is shown on the fish's body, and suffixes are shown on fish tails (see illustration opposite).

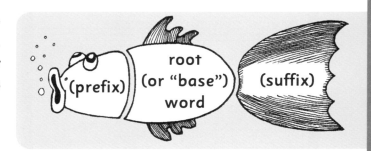

Spelling and Grammar Lessons

For each lesson, there is an activity page in the *Student Book* for the students to complete and an accompanying lesson plan in the *Teacher's Book*. The recommendations in the teacher's lesson plans are intended to be followed systematically. However, if a suggestion seems inappropriate for a particular class situation, it can of course be adapted to suit. Each lesson plan also features a reduced copy of the relevant activity page in the *Student Book*. It can be helpful to refer to this prior to, or during, the lesson.

Grammar Lessons

Each grammar lesson has its own particular focus and the lesson plans vary accordingly. Despite this, the grammar lessons all follow the same standard format, which helps to give them a recognizable shape. The format of the grammar lessons is as follows.

    a. Aim

    b. Introduction

    c. Main Point

    d. Activity Page

    e. Extension Activity

    f. Finishing the Lesson

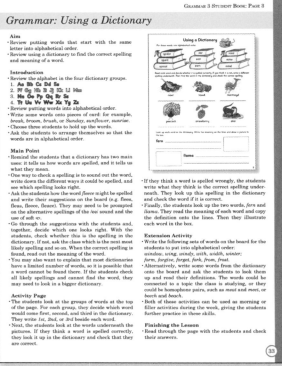

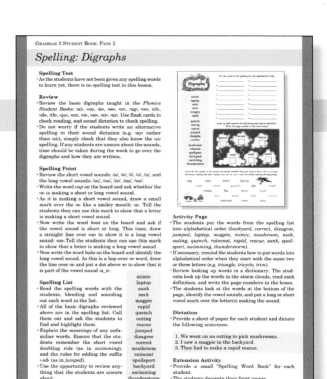

Spelling Lessons

The spelling lessons all follow the same basic format:

a. Spelling Test

b. Review

c. Spelling Point

d. Spelling List

e. Activity Page

f. Dictation

g. Extension Activity

Many teaching points are common to all of the spelling lessons, so these are explained in further detail on the following pages.

a. Spelling Test

Six pages have been provided at the back of the *Grammar 3 Student Book* for the students' spelling tests (pages 74 to 79). Start by telling the students to turn to the back of their books and find the space for that particular week's spelling test. Call out the words one at a time for the students to write on the lines. Repeat each word twice, giving the students just enough time to write each word before moving on to the next one. The words can be called out in the same order as they appear in the list, but it is best if they are called out in a random order. Those students who are finding it difficult can be given fewer words to learn.

b. Review

Each lesson should start with a short review session. To begin with, the review sessions concentrate on the five vowel letters, specifically their short and long sounds and their main alternative spellings. This can be carried out using "vowel hands" (see pages 23 to 24, Identifying the Short Vowels) and either flash cards or the *Jolly Phonics Alternative Spelling Poster*. Over the course of the year, teachers can add other areas to these review sessions, including the spelling patterns introduced or reviewed in recent lessons. A list of suitable words is suggested, which can be written on the board and discussed with the class.

c. Spelling Point

A number of the spelling lessons in the *Grammar 3 Student Book* introduce a completely new spelling pattern. However, the majority of the lessons are concerned with refining the students' spelling ability by reviewing the alternative spellings covered so far and by introducing further alternatives. There is a particular focus on expanding and consolidating the students' knowledge of the vowel sounds and their many alternative spellings. The students learn that the single vowel letters can also make the long vowel sounds, as in the words *taste, secret, child, only,* and *menu*. It is a good idea to compile a list of words for each spelling pattern with the students. The table below provides a small number of suitable words, which can be used as a starting point.

Student Book page	Word bank
2. Digraphs	*toothbrush, slither, short, boiling, argue, quail, cheek, throat, sprout, tied, shook*
4. ‹ai›, ‹ay›, ‹a_e›	*afraid, brainstorm, maintain; stingray, away, holiday; imitate, amaze, mistake*
6. ‹ee›, ‹ea›, ‹e_e›	*beekeeper, chimpanzee, creep; eager, peanut; feast; trapeze, extreme, delete*
8. ‹ie›, ‹y›, ‹igh›, ‹i_e›	*butterflies, cried, lie; dragonfly, deny, flying; thigh, might, higher; crocodile, life, invite*
10. ‹oa›, ‹ow›, ‹o_e›	*coast, hoax, throat; marshmallow, burrow, growth; suppose, broke, spoke*
12. ‹ue›, ‹ew›, ‹u_e›	*valued, clues, glued; fewer, newest, jewels; perfume, confused, includes*
14. ‹e_e›	*millipede, centipedes, incomplete, completes, competes, theme, evening*

Student Book page	Word bank
16. ‹n› saying /ng/	plank, chipmunk, drinking, thank, chunk, blink, bunk, shrank, shrinking
18. ‹ce›, ‹ci›, ‹cy›	celebrate, century, places; acidic, pencil, velocity; literacy, bouncy, fancy
20. ‹ge›, ‹gi›, ‹gy›	forgery, charge, urgent, ginger; agile, logic, original; apology, allergy, dingy
22. ‹tch›	twitches, stopwatch, pitch, crutch, ditch, sketching, stitches, thatch, itchy
24. ‹dge›	trudges, fudge, budget, ridges, dislodge, wedge, nudged, cartridge, smudged
26. ‹-le›	needle, middle, puddle, candle, little, buckle, cycle, uncle, circle, flexible, edible
28. ‹qu›	queasy, quaver, quest, squirt, squeamish, squint, squirm, squid, quench, squelch
30. ‹s› saying /z/	music, poison, pansy, as, is, was, his, hers, theirs, reason, desert, enthusiasm
32. ‹se› and ‹ze›	appease, tease, ease, arouse, praise, please, raise; squeeze, snooze, gauze, frieze
34. ‹-less›	effortless, clueless, pointless, spotless, meaningless, hopeless, limitless, tasteless
36. ‹-able›	affordable, collectable, valuable, adorable, inflatable, notable, reliable, comfortable
38. ‹a› saying /ai/	able, table, fable, staples, ague, alienate, amiable, aphids, latest, atrium
40. ‹e› saying /ee/	premium, redo, reuse, intermediate, region, emu, evenly, nausea, creation, we, be
42. ‹i› saying /ie/	find, mind, kindness, remind, silent, finally, violet, climb, digraph, ideally, I
44. ‹o› saying /oa/	photograph, opal, vocal, tokens, totally, motor, robotic, logo, post, nobody, poetry
46. ‹-o›, ‹-os›, ‹-oes›	banjo, armadillo, disco, bongo; logos, cellos; echoes, heroes, dominoes, buffaloes
48. ‹u› saying /ue/	union, universal, united, particular, bugle, Cuban, dutiful, musical, ruin, exclusive
50. ‹aw› and ‹au›	awful, drawbridge, yawn, prawn, strawberry; applaud, author, daunted, haunt, launch
52. ‹ie› saying /ee/	cookie, mischief, menagerie, masterpiece, hygienic, retrieve, prairie, yield, thief
54. ‹y› saying /i/	gymnastics, symmetry, symphony, symptom, sycamore, cylinder, synonym, antonym
56. ‹a› saying /o/	squadron, swaddle, waffle, waltz, warrior, quandary, want, what, wallop, was
58. ‹al› saying /o/	already, almost, call, wall, halt, salt, chalk, sleepwalk, falling, talking, stalking
60. Homophones	eye, I, know, no, deer, dear, it's, its, ewe, you, son, sun, one, won, tail, tale, see, sea
62. ‹ear›, ‹ere›, ‹eer›	spearmint, beard, year; merely, severe, sphere; reindeer, mountaineer, engineer
64. ‹ure›	endure, caricature, immature, manure, purely, creature, unsure, reassure
66. ‹gn› saying /n/	campaign, realign, assignment, consignment, alignment, feigned, gnashing
68. ‹ph› and ‹gh›	alphabet, catastrophe, digraph, atmosphere; trough, toughest, laughing, rougher
70. ‹air›, ‹are›, ‹ear›, ‹ere›	impaired, upstairs; dare, beware; nowhere, where; bearings, underwear
72. ‹ex›	exactly, exaggerate, excavate, extreme, exchange, exclude, exist, expand, extinct

These words could also be used as the starting point for the students' word lists in their "Spelling Word Books" (see: g. Extension Activity, page 30).

d. Spelling List

Each week, the students are given eighteen words with a particular spelling pattern to learn for a test. It is a good idea to give the spelling homework at the beginning of the week and to test at the end of the week, or on the following Monday.

The spelling words have been carefully selected to enable every student to have some success. The eighteen words are arranged on the *Student Book* pages in three groups of six. The words in the first group are usually short, regular, and fairly common; those in the second group are a bit longer and may have more alternative spellings in them; and the third group has longer, often less common words, with more varied spellings.

For those students who find spelling difficult, it may be appropriate to give them only the first six spelling words; the number can be increased when the students are ready. The number of spelling words given to the students is at the teacher's discretion, based on his or her knowledge of the students in the class.

It is important to go over the words during the spelling lesson. Look carefully at each spelling list with the class; discuss the meanings of any unfamiliar words, and look to see which parts of a word are regular and identify those parts that are not. The lesson plans in the *Teacher's Book* point out the words that need particular attention and suggest suitable learning strategies. The spelling activity pages will also help the students become more familiar with the words and their spellings. Go over the spelling words as often as possible during the week, ideally, blending and sounding out the words with the students every day.

Each student takes the list of spellings home to learn. If the students usually leave their *Student Books* at school, the words can be copied out into a small homework book for the students to take home. If the students do the writing, check that they have copied the words clearly and accurately before the books go home.

Test and grade the spellings each week. The results should be written in the students' *Student Books* for the parents to see. The grades can be shown either as a mark out of eighteen, or with a coded system if preferred. For example, a colored star system might be used, with a gold star for 18/18, a silver star for 17/18, and a colored star for 16/18. Most parents like to be involved in their children's homework, and are interested to see how many words their child spelled correctly and which words were misspelled.

Students need to be aware that accurate spelling is important for their future. Unfortunately, there is no magic wand that can be waved to make them good at spelling. In addition to knowing the letter sounds and alternative spellings thoroughly, a certain amount of dedication and practice is needed.

e. Activity Page

The focus of each spelling page reflects the main teaching point. Every week, the first of the activities requires the students to use the words from the spelling list. The students could, for example, be asked to put the spelling words into alphabetical order, to illustrate some of the words, to fill in missing letters, to complete a word search or a crossword, or to match the words to their descriptions. These activities allow the students to engage actively with the spelling words, which makes learning the words more meaningful.

The second activity requires the students to look up six words in a dictionary. At first, they are simply required to read the definition and write down the number of the page on which they found the word, but later they can be asked to write down the meaning or use the word in a sentence. Regular practice using a dictionary enables the students to find words easily and speedily. As a result, the students are more likely to use a dictionary when needed.

From early on, the students also practice separating words into syllables, which can help to improve their spelling, particularly their spelling of longer words. The students are also given a number of simple sentences to parse (identifying the parts of speech and underlining them in the appropriate color). It is best if the students start by looking for the nouns and the verbs, as most of the other parts of speech relate to them in one way or another. For some students, simply finding the nouns and verbs may be sufficient.

f. Dictation

As a weekly exercise, dictation is useful in a number of ways. It gives the students regular practice listening for the sounds in the words they write, and is a good way of monitoring their progress. Dictation helps the students to develop their independent writing and encourages the slower writers to increase their speed. It also provides a good opportunity for the students to practice their punctuation, such as speech marks and question marks. The dictation sections in each lesson plan suggest the important things to point out to the students.

There are three sentences each week for dictation. All of the sentences review the spelling focus for that week, and may also feature spelling patterns and grammar points from previous lessons. For example, when the spelling focus is ‹ure›, the dictation sentences feature words like *adventure, creature*, and *treasure*. The dictation activities also provide the students with an opportunity to use exclamation marks in speech and write proper nouns with their capital letters.

Begin by calling out the first sentence for the students to write down. Give the students a reasonable amount of time to finish writing, but not too long, and then move on to the next sentence. The few students who have not yet finished should leave the sentence incomplete and move on. This encourages them to get up to speed. Afterward, it is important to go over the sentences with the students and discuss the spellings, grammar, and punctuation points.

g. Extension Activity

It is useful for the students to have their own little Spelling Word Book. Every week, the students can collect words with the week's spelling pattern, starting with the words from the spelling list and adding more as they think of them. They can then use their Spelling Word Book to look back at the spellings they have learned or check how they should be written. They could also work in pairs and go through the books, testing each other on the spellings.

Teaching with the Grammar 3 Student Book

The following pages provide detailed lesson plans and teaching guidance for use alongside the activity pages in the *Grammar 3 Student Book*. It is a good idea to read through the relevant teaching guidance prior to each lesson, and to prepare any additional materials that might be required.

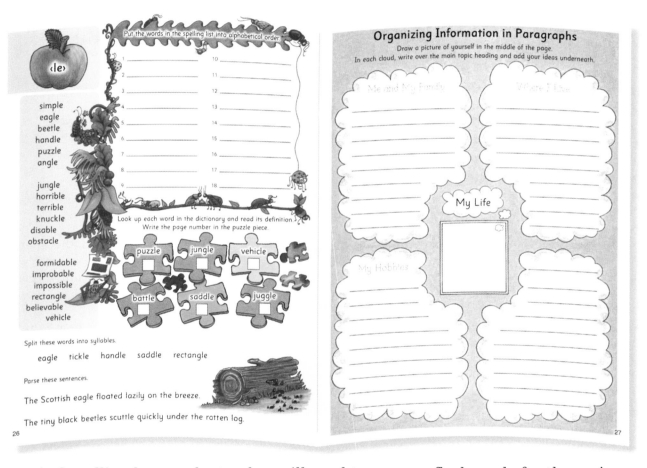

For a typical spelling lesson, the teacher will need to prepare flash cards for the review session, as well as colored pens or pencils, highlighters, paper, and dictionaries for the students' use. The teacher may also find it helpful to prepare a list of words featuring the spelling pattern(s) of the week prior to the lesson. (The word banks on pages 27 and 28 can be used as a starting point for this list.) The requirements for the grammar lessons are more varied. As for the spelling lessons, every grammar lesson requires the students to have access to dictionaries, thesauruses, and colored pens or pencils. In addition, when introducing places as proper nouns (see page 51), the students need to be able to look at world atlases, and when introducing paragraphs (see pages 57 and 59) sample texts are useful. A number of the Extension Activities also require lined paper for extended writing and art and craft materials for creating wall displays.

Spelling: Digraphs

Spelling Test
- As the students have not been given any spelling words to learn yet, there is no spelling test in this lesson.

Review
- Review the basic digraphs taught in the *Phonics Student Books*: ‹ai›, ‹oa›, ‹ie›, ‹ee›, ‹or›, ‹ng›, ‹oo›, ‹ch›, ‹sh›, ‹th›, ‹qu›, ‹ou›, ‹oi›, ‹ue›, ‹er›, ‹ar›. Use flash cards to check reading, and sound dictation to check spelling.
- Do not worry if the students write an alternative spelling in their sound dictation (e.g. ‹ay› rather than ‹ai›), simply check that they also know the ‹ai› spelling. If any students are unsure about the sounds, time should be taken during the week to go over the digraphs and how they are written.

Spelling Point
- Review the short vowel sounds: /a/, /e/, /i/, /o/, /u/, and the long vowel sounds: /ai/, /ee/, /ie/, /oa/, /ue/.
- Write the word *cap* on the board and ask whether the ‹a› is making a short or long vowel sound.
- As it is making a short vowel sound, draw a small mark over the ‹a› like a smiley mouth: ‹ă›. Tell the students they can use this mark to show that a letter is making a short vowel sound.
- Now write the word *boat* on the board and ask if the vowel sound is short or long. This time, draw a straight line over ‹oa› to show it is a long vowel sound: ‹o̅a̅›.Tell the students they can use this mark to show that a letter is making a long vowel sound.
- Now write the word *bake* on the board and identify the long vowel sound. As this is a hop-over ‹e› word, draw the line over ‹a› and put a dot above ‹e› to show that it is part of the vowel sound: ‹a̅_e̅›.

Spelling List
- Read the spelling words with the students, blending and sounding out each word in the list.
- All of the basic digraphs reviewed above are in the spelling list. Call them out and ask the students to find and highlight them.
- Explain the meanings of any unfamiliar words. Ensure that the students remember the short vowel doubling rule (as in *swimming*), and the rules for adding the suffix ‹-ed› (as in *jumped*).
- Use the opportunity to review anything that the students are unsure about.

Spelling List
mimic
laptop
sank
neck
magpie
rapid
quench
outing
rescue
jumped
disagree
correct
mushroom
raincoat
spoilsport
backyard
swimming
thunderstorm

Activity Page
- The students put the words from the spelling list into alphabetical order (*backyard, correct, disagree, jumped, laptop, magpie, mimic, mushroom, neck, outing, quench, raincoat, rapid, rescue, sank, spoilsport, swimming, thunderstorm*).
- If necessary, remind the students how to put words into alphabetical order when they start with the same two or three letters (e.g. *triangle, tricycle, trim*).
- Review looking up words in a dictionary. The students look up the words in the storm clouds, read each definition, and write the page numbers in the boxes.
- The students look at the words at the bottom of the page, identify the vowel sounds, and put a long or short vowel mark over the letter(s) making the sound.

Dictation
- Provide a sheet of paper for each student and dictate the following sentences:

1. We went on an outing to pick mushrooms.
2. I saw a magpie in the backyard.
3. They had to make a rapid rescue.

Extension Activity
- Provide a small "Spelling Word Book" for each student.
- The students decorate their front covers.

Grammar: Using a Dictionary

Aim
- Review putting words that start with the same letter into alphabetical order.
- Review using a dictionary to find the correct spelling and meaning of a word.

Introduction
- Review the alphabet in the four dictionary groups.
  1. Aa Bb Cc Dd Ee
  2. Ff Gg Hh Ii Jj Kk Ll Mm
  3. Nn Oo Pp Qq Rr Ss
  4. Tt Uu Vv Ww Xx Yy Zz
- Review putting words into alphabetical order.
- Write some words onto pieces of card: for example, *break, broom, brush,* or *Sunday, sunflower, sunrise.*
- Choose three students to hold up the words.
- Ask the students to arrange themselves so that the words are in alphabetical order.

Main Point
- Remind the students that a dictionary has two main uses: it tells us how words are spelled, and it tells us what they mean.
- One way to check a spelling is to sound out the word, write down the different ways it could be spelled, and see which spelling looks right.
- Ask the students how the word *fleece* might be spelled and write their suggestions on the board (e.g. flees, fleas, fleece, fleace). They may need to be prompted on the alternative spellings of the /ee/ sound and the use of soft ‹c›.
- Go through the suggestions with the students and, together, decide which one looks right. With the students, check whether this is the spelling in the dictionary. If not, ask the class which is the next most likely spelling and so on. When the correct spelling is found, read out the meaning of the word.
- You may also want to explain that most dictionaries have a limited number of words, so it is possible that a word cannot be found there. If the students check all likely spellings and cannot find the word, they may need to look in a bigger dictionary.

Activity Page
- The students look at the groups of words at the top of the page. For each group, they decide which word would come first, second, and third in the dictionary. They write *1st, 2nd,* or *3rd* beside each word.
- Next, the students look at the words underneath the pictures. If they think a word is spelled correctly, they look it up in the dictionary and check that they are correct.

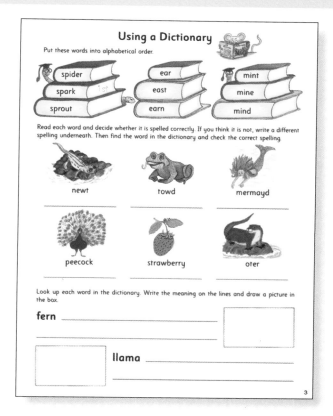

- If they think a word is spelled wrongly, the students write what they think is the correct spelling underneath. They look up this spelling in the dictionary and mark the word with a check if it is correct.
- Finally, the students look up the two words, *fern* and *llama.* They read the meaning of each word and copy the definition onto the lines. Then they illustrate each word in the box.

Extension Activity
- Write the following sets of words on the board for the students to put into alphabetical order:
  window, wing, windy, with, width, winter;
  form, forgive, forget, fork, from, frost.
- Alternatively, write some words from the dictionary onto the board and ask the students to look them up and read their definitions. The words could be connected to a topic the class is studying, or they could be homophone pairs, such as *meat* and *meet,* or *beech* and *beach.*
- Both of these activities can be used as morning or filler activities during the week, giving the students further practice in these skills.

Finishing the Lesson
- Read through the page with the students and check their answers.

33

Spelling: ⟨ai⟩, ⟨ay⟩, and ⟨a_e⟩

Spelling Test
- The students turn to the backs of their books and find the column labeled *Spelling Test 1*.
- In any order, call out the spelling words learned last week. The students write the words on the lines.

Review
- Use the "vowel hand" (see page 24) to review the five vowel letters and their short and long sounds (/a/, /e/, /i/, /o/, /u/ and /ai/, /ee/, /ie/, /oa/, /ue/).
- Next review the main alternative spellings for the long vowel sounds: ⟨ai⟩, ⟨ay⟩, ⟨a_e⟩; ⟨ee⟩, ⟨ea⟩, ⟨e_e⟩; ⟨ie⟩, ⟨y⟩, ⟨igh⟩, ⟨i_e⟩; ⟨oa⟩, ⟨ow⟩, ⟨o_e⟩; ⟨ue⟩, ⟨ew⟩, ⟨u_e⟩. This can be done with flash cards or with the *Alternative Spelling Poster*.

Spelling Point
- Review the main ways of writing the /ai/ sound and write them on the board: ⟨ai⟩, ⟨ay⟩, ⟨a_e⟩.
- Remind the students that the ⟨ay⟩ spelling is most often used at the end of words, although there are exceptions (e.g. *crayon*).
- Ask the students if they can think of any other ways to write /ai/. They might remember ⟨ei⟩ (as in *vein, reindeer, veil, reins*) and ⟨eigh⟩ (as in *eighteen, sleigh, neigh, weight*) from the *Grammar 2 Student Book*.
- Add ⟨ei⟩ and ⟨eigh⟩ to the board and ask the students to suggest words for each alternative spelling. If they suggest words with another spelling of the /ai/ sound (e.g. ⟨a⟩ as in *apron*), make another list on the board.

Spelling List
- Read the spelling words with the students, blending and sounding out each word in the list.
- With the class, identify the letters making the /ai/ sound in each word. The students highlight the letters and put the long vowel mark over them.
- Explain the meanings of any unfamiliar words. Point out the different spellings of *mail* and *male* and discuss their different meanings.
- Explain that the ⟨ay⟩ spelling is used in *praying* and *layer*, because the /ai/ sound is on the end of the root words *pray* and *lay* before the suffixes ⟨-ing⟩ and ⟨-er⟩ are added.
- It may help the students to remember which alternative spelling

stay
tail
mail
male
spray
shape
crayon
praying
mainly
layer
escape
pancake
birthday
yesterday
waiting
ailing
animate
decade

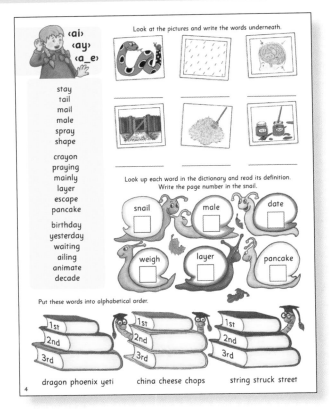

to use if the words are put together in a silly sentence: for example,

I was mainly ailing while I was waiting, then I found a tail in my mail.

Activity Page
- The students look at the pictures and write the words underneath (*snake, rain, brain, gate, hay, paint*), deciding which alternative spelling to use.
- Next, the students use a dictionary to look up the words in the snails. They read each definition and write the page numbers in the boxes.
- Finally, the students look at each set of words at the bottom of the page, and copy them out in alphabetical order in the books.

Dictation
- Provide a sheet of paper for each student and dictate the following sentences:

1. I was waiting for my mail.
2. He makes a cake of clay.
3. The boy was in the playpen.

Extension Activity
- Write the three main /ai/ spellings on the board: ⟨ai⟩, ⟨ay⟩, ⟨a_e⟩. In their Spelling Word Books, the students make a list of words for each particular spelling.

Grammar: Parts of Speech and Parsing

Aim
- Review all of the parts of speech learned in the previous two years (nouns, pronouns, adjectives, verbs, adverbs, conjunctions, and prepositions).
- Remind the students how to identify these parts of speech in a piece of writing (parsing).

Introduction
- Begin by reviewing verbs and nouns.
- Remind the class that verbs are "doing words," which can describe the past, present, and future. The color for verbs is red.
- Proper nouns start with a capital letter and are the specific names given to a particular person, place, date, or thing. All nouns that are not specific names or titles are common nouns. The color for all types of noun is black.
- Call out a word and ask the students to decide whether it is a verb or a noun, giving their answer by doing the appropriate action.
- Review the other parts of speech: pronouns (pink), adjectives (blue), adverbs (orange), conjunctions (purple), and prepositions (green). Remember to include the possessive adjectives (*my, your, his, her, its, our, your, their*). See pages 6 to 14, for more information.

Main Point
- Identifying the different parts of speech in a sentence is called *parsing*.
- Write the first sentence from the *Student Book* page on the board.
- Ask one student to identify all of the nouns and underline them in black. Then ask another student to identify the verbs and underline them in red. (It should now be easier to find the adjectives and adverbs.)
- Continue identifying the other parts of speech in the same way.
- Only two words should not be underlined: *the* and *a*.
- Explain that *the* is called the *definite article* and is used to refer to a particular thing (e.g. **the** *table in my hall*). *A* is called the *indefinite article* and refers to something in general (e.g. **a** *table has four legs*).
- Write the next sentence on the board and point out the words *she* and *her*.
- Ask the students which part of speech *she* is. (It is a pronoun, as *she* is taking the place of the noun, *Inky*.) Underline *she* in pink, and then ask which part of speech *her* is. It is a possessive adjective, as it describes whose friend Bee is, so it should be underlined in blue.

Identify as many of the different parts of speech as you can and underline them in the correct colors.

Snake's Surprise

Inky skipped happily down the dusty road and over a low bridge. She saw her friend Bee in the big meadow. Bee buzzed busily while she flew from flower to flower. Inky called, "Bee," loudly and waved, so her friend zoomed quickly across the meadow.

They walked into the forest and saw Snake. He slithered slowly among the trees toward his friends. They watched as he put a square box carefully on the bumpy ground.

"Is it a present for Inky?" Bee asked excitedly.

"I have yummy cakes for tea because it is a special day," hissed Snake.

"A special day?" repeated Bee and Inky.

"I played my drum and passed my exam. I am a good drummer!" exclaimed Snake with a big grin.

Activity Page
- Read the story with the class.
- The students underline all the nouns they can find in black. They do the same for verbs in red, and so on.

Extension Activity
- The students look at the verbs and decide whether they are in the past, present, or future.

Finishing the Lesson
- Read through the page with the students and check their answers. (See answers below. The key for the parts of speech colors is on page 17.)

Inky skipped happily down the dusty road and over a low bridge. She saw her friend Bee in the big meadow. Bee buzzed busily while she flew from flower to flower. Inky called, "Bee," loudly and waved, so her friend zoomed quickly across the meadow.

They walked into the forest and saw Snake. He slithered slowly among the trees toward his friends. They watched as he put a square box carefully on the bumpy ground.

"Is it a present for Inky?" Bee asked excitedly.

"I have yummy cakes for tea because it is a special day," hissed Snake.

"A special day?" repeated Bee and Inky.

"I played my drum and passed my exam. I am a good drummer!" exclaimed Snake with a big grin.

Spelling: ‹ee›, ‹ea›, and ‹e_e›

Spelling Test
- The students turn to the backs of their books and find the column labeled *Spelling Test 2*.
- In any order, call out the spelling words learned last week. The students write the words on the lines.

Review
- Use the "vowel hand" (see page 24) to review the five vowel letters and their short and long sounds (/a/, /e/, /i/, /o/, /u/ and /ai/, /ee/, /ie/, /oa/, /ue/).
- Next review the main alternative spellings for the long vowel sounds: ‹ai›, ‹ay›, ‹a_e›; ‹ee›, ‹ea›, ‹e_e›; ‹ie›, ‹y›, ‹igh›, ‹i_e›; ‹oa›, ‹ow›, ‹o_e›; ‹ue›, ‹ew›, ‹u_e›. This can be done with flash cards or with the *Alternative Spelling Poster*.

Spelling Point
- Review the main ways of writing the /ee/ sound and write them on the board: ‹ee›, ‹ea›, ‹e_e›.
- Ask the students if they can think of any other ways to write /ee/, such as ‹y› at the end of a word, as in *funny*. They might also remember ‹ey› (as in *key, honey, money, donkey*), and ‹ie› (as in *field, piece, shield, belief*) from the *Grammar 2 Student Book*.
- Add ‹y›, ‹ey›, and ‹ie› to the board and ask the students to suggest words for each alternative spelling. If they suggest words with another spelling of the /ee/ sound (e.g. ‹e› as in *secret*), make another list on the board.

Spelling List
- Read the spelling words with the students, blending and sounding out each word in the list.
- With the class, identify the letters making the /ee/ sound in each word. The students highlight the letters and put the long vowel mark over them.
- Explain the meanings of any unfamiliar words.
- Point out the ‹ir› spelling in *thirteen*, the ‹al› spelling in *beanstalk*, and the ‹ay› spelling in *daydream*.
- It may help the students to remember which alternative spelling to use if the words are put together in a silly sentence: for example, *The teacher daydreamed that she reached the neat beach and found a teapot full of seaweed underneath a beanstalk.*

reef
greed
neat
reach
eve
beach
teacher
theme
coffee
teapot
thirteen
evening
beanstalk
underneath
agreement
seaweed
compete
daydream

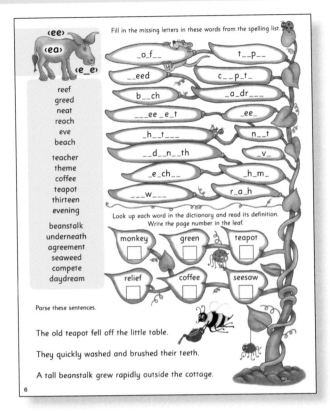

Activity Page
- The students complete the words from the spelling list (in the beans) by writing in the missing letters.
- Next, the students use a dictionary to look up the words in the leaves. They read each definition and write the page numbers in the boxes.
- Finally, the students parse the sentences, underlining each part of speech in the correct color.
  The old teapot fell off the little table.
  They quickly washed and brushed their teeth.
  A tall beanstalk grew rapidly outside the cottage.

Dictation
- Provide a sheet of paper for each student and dictate the following sentences:

1. This evening I had meat and leeks for dinner.
2. We found green seaweed on the beach.
3. I had a dream about three geese eating beans.

Extension Activity
- Write the three main /ee/ spellings on the board: ‹ee›, ‹ea›, ‹e_e›. In their Spelling Word Books, the students make a list of words for each particular spelling. They then do the same for the other alternative spellings of the /ee/ sound: ‹y›, ‹ey›, ‹ie›.

Grammar: *The Simple Tenses*

Aim
- Reinforce the students' knowledge that verbs can describe the past, present, and future.
- Introduce the term *simple tenses*. (See the section on verbs, pages 9 to 11).

Introduction
- Review verbs. Verbs are "doing words."
- Call out some words (a mixture of verbs and other words) and ask the class whether they are verbs or not. Encourage the students to do the verbs action (moving their arms backward and forward at their sides, as if running) when a verb is called out.
- Remind the students that if they can put the word *to* before a word, then it is probably a verb. When a verb is in this form (e.g. *to hop, to smile, to write*) it is called the infinitive.
- Remind the students that some words can function as more than one part of speech within a sentence; they need to look at the context and see how the word is being used (e.g. *brush* can be a noun, as in *my new brush* or a verb, as in *I brush my hair*).

Main Point
- Verbs can describe what is happening in the past, present, or future.
- The past tense of a regular verb is made by adding ‹-ed› to the verb root. There are rules for adding this suffix, depending on how the verb root is spelled:
  a. If the verb root ends with a consonant that is not immediately preceded by a short vowel, simply add ‹-ed›. So, *look* becomes *looked*.
  b. If the verb root ends in ‹e›, remove it before adding ‹-ed›. So, *smile* becomes *smiled*.
  c. If the verb root ends with a consonant that is immediately preceded by a short, stressed vowel sound, double the final consonant before adding ‹-ed›. So, *hum* becomes *hummed*.
  d. If the verb root ends in ‹y›, there are two options. When the letter before the ‹y› is a vowel, simply add ‹-ed›. So, *annoy* becomes *annoyed*. If the letter before the ‹y› is a consonant, replace the ‹y› with ‹i› before adding ‹-ed›. So, *empty* becomes *emptied*.
- The present tense is formed using the verb root without a suffix, aside from the third person singular, when ‹-s› is added. So we say, *I cook* and *you cook* but *he/she/it cooks*.
- The future is formed by adding an auxiliary verb (*shall* or *will*) before the main verb, for example, *I shall cook, you will cook, he/she/it will cook, we shall cook, you will cook, they will cook*.
- Remind the students that it helps to think of the

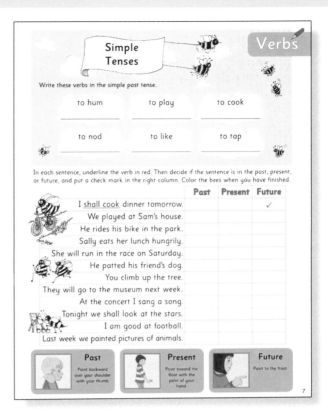

tenses in terms of actions happening yesterday (past), today (present), or tomorrow (future).
- Tell the students that the tenses they have learned so far are called the *simple tenses*.
- Write some verbs on the board (e.g. *hop, play, help, bake*). As a class, decide how to form each verb in the past tense (*hopped, played, helped, baked*). Alternatively, choose some students to do this individually.
- Call out some sentences. Ask the class to decide whether they are in the past, present, or future, and do the right action (as shown on the *Student Book* page).

Activity Page
- The students look at each verb and write it in the simple past tense, remembering to apply the appropriate spelling rule.
- Next, they read the sentences and underline the verbs in red. Remind the students that for verbs written in the simple future, they should underline the auxiliary verb (*shall* or *will*) as well as the main verb.
- Finally, they identify which tense each sentence is written in and put a check mark in the *past, present*, or *future* column.

Extension Activity
- Write the following sentence on the board: *I brush my hair*. Ask the students to copy it out and then write it in the simple past and the simple future.

Spelling: ‹ie›, ‹y›, ‹igh›, and ‹i_e›

Spelling Test
- The students turn to the backs of their books and find the column labeled *Spelling Test 3*.
- In any order, call out the spelling words learned last week. The students write the words on the lines.

Review
- Use the "vowel hand" (see page 24) to review the five vowel letters and their short and long sounds (/a/, /e/, /i/, /o/, /u/ and /ai/, /ee/, /ie/, /oa/, /ue/).
- Review the main alternative spellings for the long vowel sounds: ‹ai›, ‹ay›, ‹a_e›; ‹ee›, ‹ea›, ‹e_e›; ‹ie›, ‹y›, ‹igh›, ‹i_e›; ‹oa›, ‹ow›, ‹o_e›; ‹ue›, ‹ew›, ‹u_e›. This can be done with flash cards or with the *Alternative Spelling Poster*.

Spelling Point
- Review the main ways of writing the /ie/ sound and write them on the board: ‹ie›, ‹y›, ‹igh›, ‹i_e›.
- Ask the students to suggest words for each alternative spelling. If they suggest a word with another spelling of the /ie/ sound (e.g. ‹i› as in *child*), make another list on the board.

Spelling List
- Read the spelling words with the students, blending and sounding out each word in the list.
- With the class, identify the letters making the /ie/ sound in each word. The students highlight the letters and put the long vowel mark over them.
- Explain the meanings of any unfamiliar words.
- Point out that the word *alright* only has one ‹l›, and that *lightning* only has ‹n› before the ‹ing› whereas *frightening* has ‹en›.
- The plural word *flies* follows the spelling rule of replacing ‹y› with "shy ‹i›" before adding ‹-es›.
- It may help the students to remember which alternative spelling to use if the words are put together in a silly sentence: for example, *I'm highly delighted as the lightning is frightening, alright?*

life
high
flies
spying
dive
tied
dryer
tried
alright
firework
alive
delight
describe
asylum
lightning
frightening
butterfly
pantomime

Activity Page
- The students find the words from the spelling list in the word search and work out which word is missing (*asylum*).

- Next, the students use a dictionary to look up the words in the dice. They read each definition and write the page numbers in the boxes.
- Finally, the students parse the sentences, underlining each part of speech in the correct color.
Granny makes a tasty pie.
The brave knight swiftly rescued the princess.
The black and white magpie flies in the blue sky.

Dictation
- Provide a sheet of paper for each student and dictate the sentences below. Remind the students that the third sentence needs a question mark.

1. The piebald horse did not like flies.
2. I might have a ride on my bike.
3. Can the sharp knife cut the plywood?

Extension Activity
- Write the main /ie/ spellings on the board: ‹ie›, ‹y›, ‹igh›, and ‹i_e›. In their Spelling Word Books, the students make a list of words for each particular spelling.
- The students can then do the same for any other alternative spellings of the /ie/ sound.

Grammar: Verbs Ending in ‹-y› *(and the Third Person Singular)*

Aim
- Refine the students' knowledge of how a verb ending in ‹y› forms the third person singular.

Introduction
- Review the personal pronouns and their actions. (I: point to yourself; you: point to someone else; he/she/it: point to a boy/a girl/the floor; we: point in a circle, including yourself and others; you: point to two other people; they: point to the class next door.)
- Remind the students that the first *you* is singular and the second is plural.
- Choose a regular verb and conjugate it aloud with the students (e.g. *I cook, you cook, he/she/it cooks, we cook, you cook, they cook*), doing the pronoun actions together. Then conjugate the same verb in the simple past tense (*I cooked, you cooked*, and so on) and the simple future (*I shall cook, you will cook*, and so on).

Main Point
- Remind the class that when *I, you,* and *he/she/it* are put before a verb, they are called the first, second, and third person singular. Similarly, *we, you,* and *they* are the first, second, and third person plural.
- Remind the students that when they conjugate a regular verb in the present tense, they must add a suffix to the verb root to make the third person singular. This is usually ‹-s› (e.g. *he/she/it cooks*), but can sometimes be ‹-es›, depending on how the verb root is spelled:
- If the verb root ends in ‹sh›, ‹ch›, ‹s›, ‹z›, or ‹x›, add ‹-es› (e.g. *he brushes, she munches, it hisses, it fizzes, she fixes*). This idea should be familiar to the students as the same rule applies to making plural nouns.
- If the verb root ends in a ‹y› that is immediately preceded by a consonant, replace the ‹y› with ‹i› before adding ‹-es› (e.g. *dry* becomes *dries*). Other such examples include: *to apply, to bury, to copy, to defy, to deny, to empty, to envy, to ferry, to fly, to fry, to identify, to imply, to marry, to pity, to pry, to rely, to satisfy, to vary.*
- However, if the verb root ends in a ‹y› that is immediately preceded by a vowel, simply add ‹-s› (e.g. *stray* becomes *strays*). Other such examples include: *to betray, to decay, to delay, to obey, to pray, to toy.*
- Explain that extra care needs to be taken when writing the third person singular of verbs ending in ‹y›. The students will not be able to tell which suffix to use by listening to the word; they have to use the spelling rules.

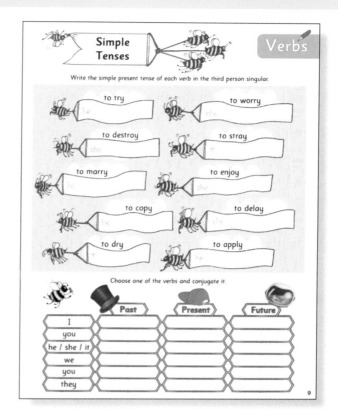

Activity Page
- The students write inside the outlined word *Verbs*, using a red pencil.
- They look at each verb in turn and write it in the third person singular of the simple present tense, remembering to apply the appropriate spelling rule (*he tries, she worries, she destroys,* and so on).
- Next, they choose one of the verbs from the clouds and conjugate it in the past, present, and future, at the bottom of the page.

Extension Activity
- The students conjugate another verb ending in ‹y› in the past, present, and future.
- They draw a picture to illustrate their verb.

Finishing the Lesson
- Read through the page with the students and check their answers.

Spelling: ‹oa›, ‹ow›, and ‹o_e›

Spelling Test
- The students turn to the backs of their books and find the column labeled *Spelling Test 4*.
- In any order, call out the spelling words learned last week. The students write the words on the lines.

Review
- Use the "vowel hand" (see page 24) to review the five vowel letters and their short and long sounds (/a/, /e/, /i/, /o/, /u/ and /ai/, /ee/, /ie/, /oa/, /ue/).
- Review the main alternative spellings for the long vowel sounds: ‹ai›, ‹ay›, ‹a_e›; ‹ee›, ‹ea›, ‹e_e›; ‹ie›, ‹y›, ‹igh›, ‹i_e›; ‹oa›, ‹ow›, ‹o_e›; ‹ue›, ‹ew›, ‹u_e›. This can be done with flash cards or with the *Alternative Spelling Poster*.

Spelling Point
- Review the main ways of writing the /oa/ sound and write them on the board: ‹oa›, ‹ow›, ‹o_e›.
- Remind the students that the ‹ow› spelling is most often used at the end of words; although there are exceptions (e.g. *own*).
- Ask the students to suggest words for each alternative spelling. If they suggest words with another spelling of the /oa/ sound (e.g. ‹o› as in *only*), make another list on the board.

Spelling List
- Read the spelling words with the students, blending and sounding out each word in the list.
- With the class, identify the letters making the /oa/ sound in each word. The students highlight the letters and put the long vowel mark over them. Explain the meanings of any unfamiliar words.
- Point out the ‹igh› spelling in *tightrope*, and the ‹ck› spelling after the short vowel sound in *cockroach*.
- Explain that the ‹ow› spelling in *slowest* appears in the middle because the root word *slow* has had the suffix ‹-est› added to it.
- It may help the students to remember which alternative spelling to use if the words are put together in a silly sentence: for example, *The floating cockroach approached the moaning, croaking toad.*

float
joke
croak
elbow
owner
alone
follow
explode
homework
moaning
shadow
slowest
rainbow
approach
tightrope
cockroach
hormone
envelope

Activity Page
- The students read the phrases and decide which words from the spelling list they describe.

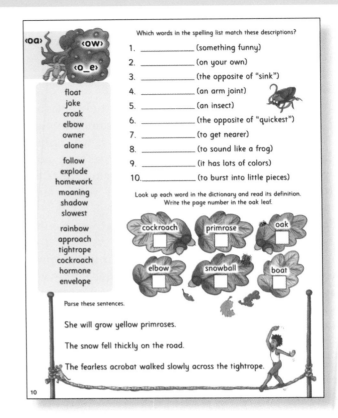

- Next, the students use a dictionary to look up the words in the oak leaves. They read each definition and write the page numbers in the boxes.
- Finally, the students parse the sentences, underlining each part of speech in the correct color. Remind them that the first sentence is written in the simple future, so the auxiliary verb (*will*) should be underlined in red along with the main verb (*grow*).

  She will grow yellow primroses.
  The snow fell thickly on the road.
  The fearless acrobat walked slowly across the tightrope.

Dictation
- Provide a sheet of paper for each student and dictate the sentences below. Remind the students that the third sentence needs a question mark.

  1. The foal ran across the road.
  2. They baked homemade cake for tea.
  3. Is the boat made of oak?

Extension Activity
- Write the main /ie/ spellings on the board: ‹ie›, ‹y›, ‹igh›, and ‹i_e›. In their Spelling Word Books, the students make a list of words for each particular spelling.

Grammar: The Verb "to be" *(in Past, Present, and Future)*

Aim
- Review the simple past and simple present tenses of the irregular verb *to be,* and introduce the simple future of the verb.

Introduction
- Remind the students that some verbs do not form the past tense by adding ‹-ed› to the root. Instead, the roots of these verbs change when they are put into the past. These are called irregular past tenses or "tricky pasts."
- Review some tricky pasts with the students; call out some examples and ask the students to give you the infinitive, or call out the infinitive and ask them to give you the tricky past. For example, *I won (to win),* or *to sing, (I sang)* and so on.
- Other examples include: *to drink/drank, to lose/lost, to ride/rode, to say/said, to speak/spoke, to run/ran, to dig/dug, to hide/hid, to make/made, to ring/rang, to throw/threw, to write/wrote.*

Main Point
- The verb *to be* is very irregular in the past and present tenses. As a result, students often find it difficult to identify as a verb in a sentence. However, it is important for the students to overcome this problem as *to be* is one of the most frequently used verbs. It is also used to form other tenses, such as the past, present, and future continuous (e.g. *I was sitting, I am sitting, I shall be sitting*).
- Starting with the present tense, conjugate the verb *to be* as a class and write it on the board. Then do the same for the past tense.
- Now, see if the students can give each part of the verb *to be* in the simple future, which is formed in the regular way with the auxiliary *shall* or *will* before the main verb. (*Will* can be used with all of the pronouns, but *shall* is only used with *I* and *we*.)
- Write each part on the board as they work it out, and point out that although it is irregular in the past and present tenses, it is regular in the future.

Past	Present	Future
I was	I am	I shall be
you were	you are	you will be
he/she/it was	he/she/it is	he/she/it will be
we were	we are	we shall be
you were	you are	you will be
they were	they are	they will be

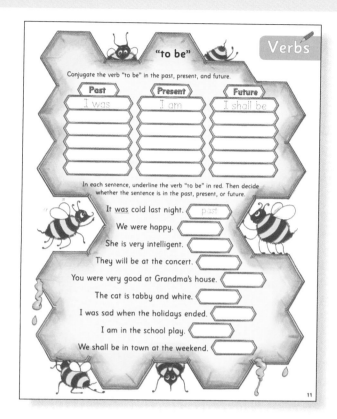

- Now write some sentences on the board, using the verb *to be* in the past, present, and future, and ask the students to identify the verb in each of them.
- Example sentences include: *We were on the bus*; *She is happy; They are cold; You will be seven.*
- Remind the students that these are all examples of the simple tenses.

Activity Page
- The students write inside the outlined word *Verbs,* using a red pencil. They conjugate the verb *to be* in the simple past, present, and future.
- Next they identify the verb *to be* in each sentence, underlining it in red (they should also underline the auxiliary *shall* or *will* in the simple future).
- Finally, they decide whether each verb is in the past, present, or future, and write the correct tense in the honeycomb.

Extension Activity
- Ask the students to write some sentences of their own, using the verb *to be.*
- Ask them to say whether their sentences are in the past, present, or future.

Finishing the Lesson
- Read through the page with the students and check their answers.

Spelling: ‹ue›, ‹ew›, and ‹u_e›

Spelling Test
- The students turn to the backs of their books and find the column labeled *Spelling Test 5*.
- In any order, call out the spelling words learned last week. The students write the words on the lines.

Review
- Use the "vowel hand" (see page 24) to review the five vowel letters and their short and long sounds (/a/, /e/, /i/, /o/, /u/ and /ai/, /ee/, /ie/, /oa/, /ue/).
- Review the main alternative spellings for the long vowel sounds: ‹ai›, ‹ay›, ‹a_e›; ‹ee›, ‹ea›, ‹e_e›; ‹ie›, ‹y›, ‹igh›, ‹i_e›; ‹oa›, ‹ow›, ‹o_e›; ‹ue›, ‹ew›, ‹u_e›. This can be done with flash cards or with the *Alternative Spelling Poster*.

Spelling Point
- Review the main ways of writing the /ue/ sound and write them on the board: ‹ue›, ‹ew›, ‹u_e›.
- Remind the students that these spellings can also make the long /oo/ sound, as in *blue, grew*, and *rude*.
- Ask them to suggest words for each alternative spelling. If they suggest words with another spelling of the /ue/ sound (e.g. ‹u› as in *emu*), make another list on the board.

Spelling List
- Read the spelling words with the students, blending and sounding out each word in the list.
- With the class, identify the letters making the /ue/ or /oo/ sound in each word. The students highlight the letters and put the long vowel mark over them.
- Explain the meanings of any unfamiliar words.
- Point out that *Yuletide* has a capital letter as it is a proper noun.
- It may help the students to remember which alternative spelling to use if the words are put together in a silly sentence: for example, *The newts threw fewer screwdrivers.*
- It is a good idea to blend and sound out the spelling words quickly every day with the students.

cue
flute
amuse
statue
threw
fewer
bluebell
venue
pollute
volume
newt
fortune
Yuletide
avenue
attitude
costume
absolute
screwdriver

Activity Page
- The students fill in the crossword using the words from the spelling list. (The numbers in the crossword indicate the correct word from the spelling list.)

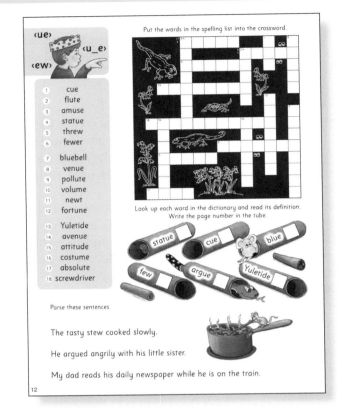

- Next, the students use a dictionary to look up the words in the tubes. They read each definition and write the page numbers in the boxes.
- Finally, the students parse the sentences, underlining each part of speech in the correct color.
  The <u>tasty</u> <u>stew</u> <u>cooked</u> <u>slowly</u>.
  He <u>argued</u> <u>angrily</u> <u>with</u> <u>his</u> <u>little</u> <u>sister</u>.
  <u>My</u> <u>dad</u> <u>reads</u> <u>his</u> <u>daily</u> <u>newspaper</u> <u>while</u> <u>he</u> <u>is</u> <u>on</u> the <u>train</u>.

Dictation
- Provide a sheet of paper for each student and dictate the sentences below. Remind the students that the second sentence needs a question mark and that *Tuesday* is a proper noun with a capital letter.

> 1. There is a huge statue in the avenue.
> 2. Can you give our excuses for Tuesday?
> 3. The firemen had to rescue a few ewes.

Extension Activity
- Write the main /ue/ spellings on the board: ‹ue›, ‹ew›, and ‹u_e›. In their Spelling Word Books, the students make a list of words for each particular spelling. They then do the same for any other alternative spellings of the /ue/ sound.

Grammar: Syllables

Aim
- Develop the students' understanding that words are made up of units of sound called *syllables*.

Introduction
- Remind the students that a compound word is a word made of two (or more) shorter words joined together.
- Ask the students to call out some compound words and write them on the board.
- Then ask the class to identify the shorter words in each one and separate them with a line (e.g. *green/ house*). Then, with the students, say each compound word in turn and clap once for every shorter word. So, for a word like *greenhouse*, there would be two claps: *green* (clap) / *house* (clap).
- Other examples include:

  oil/can,   with/out,   land/mark,
  fog/horn,   scrap/book,   rain/drop,
  milk/man,   snow/ball,   foot/step.

Main Point
- An understanding of syllables will help improve the students' spelling, particularly their spelling of longer words.
- Explain that words are made up of units of sound called *syllables* and that each syllable contains a vowel sound. Look at the compound words again with the students and identify the vowel sounds. Each shorter word contains one vowel sound and, therefore, makes one syllable.
- A syllable is not necessarily a whole word. Write the word *unkind* on the board and separate the prefix *un* with a line (*un/kind*).
- Explain that this word has two syllables or "beats" and say the word, clapping for each syllable: *un* (clap) / *kind* (clap).
- Now tell the students to rest their chin on the back of one hand and slowly say the word. Each time they say a vowel sound, their chin goes down. If they count the number of times they feel their chin go down, it will tell them how many syllables are in the word. This activity is called "chin bumps."
- Do the same with other two-syllable words with prefixes and suffixes (e.g. *wish/ing, thank/ful, non/sense*).
- Write the word *disagree* on the board and identify the vowel sounds with the students. Separate the syllables with a line and count them: *dis/a/gree*.
- Then ask the students to say the word using "chin bumps" and count the syllables that way.
- Do the same with other three-syllable words (e.g. *sev/en/teen, hand/ker/chief, wa/ter/fall, flow/er/ pot, ham/bur/ger*).

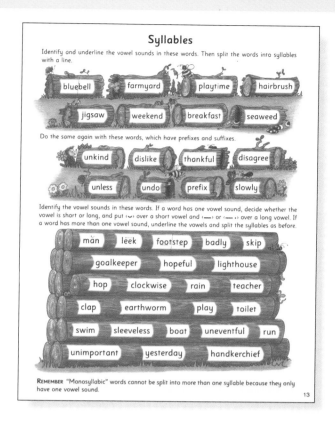

- Now write the word *ran* on the board and ask the class how many syllables it has.
- Explain that this word is monosyllabic, which means it has only one syllable, and cannot be split any further.
- Identify the vowel sound with the students and ask them whether it is a short or long vowel. Put a short vowel mark ‹˘› over the ‹a›, so it reads *răn*.
- Do the same with the word *seed*, only this time put a long vowel mark, ‹¯›, over the ‹ee›, so it reads *sēed*.

Activity Page
- In each section, the students underline the vowel sounds in the words and separate the syllables with a line.
- In the last section, the students also have to look out for monosyllabic words. If a word is monosyllabic, they decide whether its vowel sound is short: /a/, /e/, /i/, /o/, /u/, or long: /ai/, /ee/, /ie/, /oa/, /ue/, and put the appropriate symbol over the letters making the vowel sound.

Extension Activity
- Write more words on the board and ask the students to separate them into syllables.

Finishing the Lesson
- Read through the page with the students.

Spelling: ‹e_e›

Spelling Test
- The students turn to the backs of their books and find the column labeled *Spelling Test 6*.
- In any order, call out the spelling words learned last week. The students write the words on the lines.

Review
- Use the "vowel hand" (see page 24) to review the five vowel letters and their short and long sounds.
- Review the main alternative spellings for the long vowel sounds using flash cards.
- Write the following words on the board: *hail, say, came, sheep, tea, eve, tie, sky, high, kite, boat, slow, bone, cue, stew, tube.*
- Blend and sound out the words with the class, and identify the alternative spellings.

Spelling Point
- The main ways of writing the /ee/ sound are ‹ee›, ‹ea›, and ‹e_e›. Previously, the focus has been on ‹ee› and ‹ea› because the ‹e_e› spelling is mainly used in longer, more complicated words. Explain that for spelling the students should think about using ‹ee› or ‹ea› for the /ee/ sound, unless the word is long or complicated, when they should try ‹e_e›.

Spelling List
- Read the spelling words with the students, blending and sounding out each word in the list.
- Ask the students which letters are making the /ee/ sound. They highlight ‹e_e› in each word, and put the long vowel mark over the first ‹e› and a dot over the second.
- Explain the meanings of any unfamiliar words, like *phoneme*: a sound in speech. Tell the class that the phoneme common to all of the spelling words this week is /ee/.
- Point out the soft ‹g› in *gene*, and the soft ‹c› in *recede, concede,* and *centipede*. Draw attention to the ‹ch› spelling of the /k/ sound in *scheme*, the ‹u› spelling of /oo/ in *supreme*, the ‹ph› in *phoneme*, and the capital letter in *Chinese*. It may help the students to remember which alternative spelling to use if the words are put together in a silly sentence: for example, *These supreme Chinese athletes look completely serene as they compete on the trapeze.*

gene
these
recede
delete
impede
scheme
concede
stampede
complete
extreme
athlete
concrete
supreme
intervene
phoneme
Chinese
obsolete
centipede

Activity Page
- The students find the words from the spelling list in the word search and work out which word is missing (*Chinese*).
- Next, the students use a dictionary to look up the words in the theme park. They read each definition and write the page numbers in the boxes.
- Then they underline the vowel sounds in the words and separate the words into syllables with a line (*con/crete, ath/lete, ex/treme, in/ter/vene*). *These* only has one syllable, so the students add the long vowel mark.
- Finally, the students parse the sentences, underlining each part of speech in the correct color. Remind them that the first sentence is written in the simple future, so the auxiliary verb (*will*) should be underlined in red along with the main verb (*compete*).
The <u>athletes</u> <u>will compete</u> <u>in</u> the <u>morning</u>.
<u>I</u> <u>accidentally</u> <u>deleted</u> <u>my</u> <u>work</u> <u>on</u> the <u>computer</u>.

Dictation
- Provide a sheet of paper for each student and dictate the sentences below. Remind the students that *Uncle Tom* is a proper noun and needs capital letters.

1. We went to the theme park with Uncle Tom.
2. There was a loud clap of thunder which made the cows stampede.
3. The computer was so old it was obsolete.

Grammar: The Present Participle

Aim
- Refine the students' knowledge of the suffix ‹-ing›, and introduce the term *present participle*.

Introduction
- Remind the class that a suffix is usually one or more syllables added at the end of a word to change its meaning.
- Ask the students whether they can think of any suffixes they know already, such as those used to make plural nouns: ‹-s›, ‹-es›, and ‹-ies›, or those used to make comparative and superlative adjectives: ‹-er› and ‹-est›.
- Suffixes can also be used with verbs. The students know that the simple past tense of regular verbs is made by adding the suffix ‹-ed›. Remind the class that another suffix commonly used with verbs is ‹-ing›; so *walk*, for example, becomes *walking*. However, like ‹-ed›, there are rules for adding this suffix, depending on how the verb root is spelled:

a. Like ‹-ed›, if the verb root ends with a consonant that is not immediately preceded by a short vowel, simply add ‹-ing›. So, *look* becomes *looking*.

b. Like ‹-ed›, if the verb root ends in ‹e›, remove it before adding ‹-ing›. So, *smile* becomes *smiling*. The only exception is when the verb root has an ‹i› before the ‹e›, as in *die*. To avoid having two ‹i›s next to each other (as in "diing"), both ‹i› and ‹e› are replaced with ‹y›. So, *die* becomes *dying*, even though the simple past is *died*.

c. Like ‹-ed›, if the verb root ends with a consonant that is immediately preceded by a short, stressed vowel sound, double the final consonant before adding ‹-ing›. So, *nod* becomes *nodding*.

d. Unlike ‹-ed›, if a verb root ends in ‹y›, it is unimportant whether there is a vowel or consonant immediately before it: simply add ‹-ing›. So, *play* becomes *playing,* and *worry* becomes *worrying*. Although "shy ‹i›" replaces ‹y› in *worried*, it does not return in *worrying* because it would look odd having two ‹i›s next to each other.

Main Point
- English verbs have two participles: the present participle and the past participle.
- The present participle is used to form the continuous tenses, which the students will be learning in the following two grammar lessons.
- The present participle can also be used as an adjective (as in *the **winding** road*) and takes the same form as the gerund, which acts as a noun (as in ***dancing** is fun*). The students can learn about these uses when they are older.

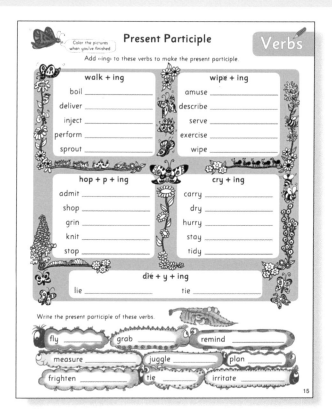

- Write the words *snap, melt, explode, cry*, and *die* on the board and ask some of the students to come and add the suffix ‹-ing› (*snapping, melting, exploding, crying, dying*). They will need to look at how the verb root is spelled, and work out which spelling rule to use before adding ‹-ing›.
- Explain that these words ending in ‹-ing› are all examples of the present participle.

Activity Page
- The students write inside the outlined word *Verbs*, using a red pencil.
- They add ‹-ing› to the verbs in each section (which are grouped according to the different spelling rules) to make the present participle.
- Lastly, the students write more present participles in the caterpillars, working out which spelling rule to use for each verb.

Extension Activity
- Write some more verbs on the board and ask the class to write down the present participle for each one.

Finishing the Lesson
- Read through the page with the students and check their answers.

Spelling: The ‹n› Spelling of the /ng/ Sound

Spelling Test
- The students turn to the backs of their books and find the column labeled *Spelling Test 7*.
- In any order, call out the spelling words learned last week. The students write the words on the lines.

Review
- Use the "vowel hand" (see page 24) to review the five vowel letters and their short and long sounds.
- Review the main alternative spellings for the long vowel sounds using flash cards.
- Write the following words on the board: *wait, away, grape, been, bean, these, pie, sty, light, bike, toad, snow, nose, due, new, cube.*
- Blend and sound out the words with the class, and identify the alternative spellings.

Spelling Point
- Review the ‹ng› spelling of the /ng/ sound.
- Remind the students that when the sounds /ng/ and /k/ come together, they are nearly always written as ‹nk›. Write the word *sunk* on the board.
- Ask for some more ‹nk› words and write them on the board (e.g. *pink, bank, honk, blink*). Ask the class which letter in these words is making the /ng/ sound.
- Very slowly, sound out *sunk*, /s-u-ng-k/, and explain that sometimes ‹n› makes the /ng/ sound on its own.
- Now write the word *anger* on the board and sound it out: /a-ng-g-er/. Here, too, it is ‹n› that makes the /ng/ sound, as the /g/ is spoken.
- Do this with some other examples (e.g. *kangaroo, longer, hunger*), writing them on the board and sounding them out with the students.

Spelling List
- Read the spelling words with the students, and ask them to highlight the ‹n› making the /ng/ sound.
- Explain the meanings of any unfamiliar words.
- Tell the students to emphasize the ‹or› in *anchor* and the ‹d› in *handkerchief* to help them with the spelling. Pay particular attention to *extinct, distinctive,* and *defunct.* In these words the /ng/ and /k/ sounds come together but they are written as ‹nc›. Ask the students what is different about the ‹nk› words and the ‹nc› words; they may notice that ‹nk› often comes at the end of a word, or is followed by a vowel sound,

anger
skunk
tanker
junk
trunk
sunken
anchor
blanket
finger
hunger
angler
extinct
stinking
handkerchief
anguish
distinctive
defunct
singular

whereas ‹nc› is always followed by a consonant.
- Care is needed with a word like *anchor*; although the /k/ sound is followed by a vowel sound, it is written as ‹ch›. Words like this are usually derived from Greek and have to be learned.

Activity Page
- The students read and illustrate each word.
- Next, the students use a dictionary to look up the words in the blankets. They read each definition and write the page numbers in the boxes.
- Then they identify the vowel sounds in the words and separate the words into syllables (*blan/ket, tan/ker, hand/ker/chief*). *Skunk* and *junk* are monosyllabic, so the students add the short vowel mark instead.
- Finally, the students parse the sentences, underlining each part of speech in the correct color.
  The Chinese junk anchored safely in the bay.
  The black and white skunk ran quickly into the wood.

Dictation
- Dictate the following sentences:

1. The boat sank in a storm.
2. I think I would like a cold drink.
3. The monkey winked at the kangaroo.

Grammar: The Present Continuous

Aim

- Develop the students' understanding of verbs and introduce the present continuous (also called the present progressive).
- Explain that the present continuous is formed by using an auxiliary verb, *to be*, followed by the present participle.

Introduction

- Review the tenses for the simple past, present, and future. Remind the students that the action of the verb is either taking place now (the present), has already happened (the past), or will happen at some time (the future).
- Call out some sentences and ask the students to do the appropriate action to show whether the sentences are in the past (pointing their thumb back over their shoulder), the present (pointing toward the floor with the palm of their hand), or the future (pointing to the front with their index finger).

Main Point

- The continuous tenses, like the simple tenses, can happen in the past, present, and future. However, they are used to convey a slightly different meaning.
- Write the following sentences on the board: *I walk to school* and *I am walking to school*.
- Ask the students what is different about the first and second sentence. They may notice a difference in meaning, but it is more likely they will see that the verb is *walk* in the first sentence, and *am walking* in the second.
- Tell the class that the first sentence is written in the simple present, but the second one is in another tense called the present continuous. Explain that the present continuous is made by adding the present participle (e.g. *walking*) to the auxiliary verb *to be*.
- With the class, conjugate the verb *to be* in the simple present (*I am, you are, he/she/it is, we are, you are, they are*), doing the pronoun actions. Underline *am* in *I am walking to school* in red on the board.
- Now conjugate the verb *to walk* in the present continuous (*I am walking, you are walking, he/she/it is walking, we are walking, you are walking, they are walking*). Underline *walking* in red on the board, so that both parts of the verb (*am walking*) are now underlined in red.
- Look at the two sentences on the board again. Explain that the **simple present** is used to describe an action that is repeated or usual (e.g. *I walk to school every day.*)
- The **present continuous** is used to describe something that has started, is continuing, and has not yet

stopped. It could describe an action happening right now (e.g. *I am walking to school*) or as a longer action in progress, but not necessarily happening at this exact moment (e.g. *I am learning to swim*). There are other uses of these tenses, but they can be taught when the students are older.

Activity Page

- The students conjugate the verb *to be* in the simple present.
- Next, they read the pairs of sentences, underlining the verbs in red and identifying which tense each sentence is written in. Remind the students to underline the auxiliary verb, *to be*, as well as the main verb.
- Finally, they read the sentences at the bottom of the page and underline the verbs in red and the pronouns in pink, before rewriting the sentences in the present continuous.

Extension Activity

- Write some more sentences on the board in the simple present, and ask the students to rewrite them in the present continuous.
- Alternatively, you could ask some of the students to do the activity using sentences of their own.

Finishing the Lesson

- Read through the page with the students.

Spelling: Soft ‹c›

Spelling Test
- The students turn to the backs of their books and find the column labeled *Spelling Test 8.*
- In any order, call out the spelling words learned last week. The students write the words on the lines.

Review
- Use the "vowel hand" (see page 24) to review the five vowel letters and their short and long sounds.
- Review the main alternative spellings for the long vowel sounds using flash cards.
- Then review the /ng/ sound and how to write it: ‹ng› as in *long, strength,* and *singing,* and ‹n› as in *drink, extinct,* and *anger.* Encourage the students to think of as many words as they can for each spelling.

Spelling Point
- Review the soft ‹c› spelling. Remind the class that when the letter ‹c› is followed by ‹e›, ‹i›, or ‹y›, it usually makes the /s/ sound (e.g. *rice, circle, icy*).
- Write ‹ce›, ‹ci›, and ‹cy› on the board and ask the students to call out as many soft ‹c› words as they can.
- Make a list of words for each spelling and identify the soft ‹c› in each word with the class.

Spelling List
- Read the spelling words with the students and identify the soft ‹c› in each one.
- Ask the class to highlight the ‹ce›, ‹ci›, or ‹cy› making the /s/ sound or draw a ring around it.
- Explain the meanings of any unfamiliar words.
- Explain that sometimes the ‹e› in ‹ce› is doing two things: it is part of the soft ‹c› spelling and it is also a "magic ‹e›," making the short vowel in front of the ‹c› into a long one (e.g. *race, space, twice*). However, in words of more than one syllable the long vowel tends to get swallowed and sounds more like /is/ (e.g. *office, palace*).
- Point out that in words like *princess, medicine,* and *vacancy,* the ‹e›, ‹i›, and ‹y› each says its own sound, as well as helping to make the ‹c› soft.
- It may help the students to remember which alternative spelling to use if the words are put together in a silly sentence: for example, *The princess in the palace likes twice as much cinnamon on her cereal.*
- It is a good idea to blend and sound out the spelling words quickly every day with the students.

race
space
since
twice
cancel
princess
office
palace
voice
silence
bounce
incident
accident
medicine
cereal
vacancy
advance
cinnamon

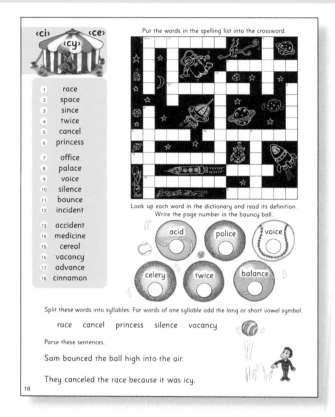

Activity Page
- The students fill in the crossword using the words from the spelling list. (The numbers in the crossword indicate the correct word from the spelling list.)
- Next, the students use a dictionary to look up the words in the bouncy balls. They read each definition and write the page numbers in the boxes.
- Then they identify the vowel sounds in the words and separate the words into syllables (*can/cel, prin/cess, si/lence, va/can/cy*). *Race* is monosyllabic, so the students add the long vowel mark instead.
- Finally, the students parse the sentences, underlining each part of speech in the correct color.
  <u>Sam</u> <u>bounced</u> the <u>ball</u> <u>high</u> <u>into</u> the <u>air</u>.
  <u>They</u> <u>canceled</u> the <u>race</u> <u>because</u> <u>it</u> <u>was</u> <u>icy</u>.

Dictation
- Provide a sheet of paper for each student and dictate the following sentences:

  1. The mice live in a nice place in the city.
  2. The ice dancers twice did a big circle on the rink.
  3. The policeman had a friendly face.

Extension Activity
- The students make a list of words for each of the soft ‹c› spellings: ‹ce›, ‹ci›, ‹cy›.

Grammar: The Past Continuous

Aim
- Develop the students' understanding of the simple and continuous tenses and introduce the past continuous (also called the past progressive).

Introduction
- Review the simple and continuous tenses covered so far.
- Draw a simple grid on the board with three boxes across the top and two boxes down, and write in the tenses as you talk about them.
- Start with the simple past, present, and future along the top row; then add the present continuous in the middle column of the bottom row. Leave room for the past continuous in the bottom-left corner.
- Discuss with the students how each tense is formed.
- Remind them that the simple present describes an action that is repeated or usual (e.g. *She plays tennis twice a week*), while the present continuous describes something that has started and is still happening (e.g. *We are playing a game*).

Main Point
- Explain that the continuous tenses, like the simple tenses, can happen in the past as well as the present.
- On the board, write *past continuous* in the bottom-left corner of the grid. Like the present continuous, the past continuous is made by adding the present participle to the auxiliary verb *to be*.
- Write these sentences on the board: *I walked to school* and *I was walking to school.*
- Look at the first sentence, and ask the students which tense is being used (the simple past) and how they know this (the verb root has the suffix ‹-ed› added to it).
- Now look at the second sentence and ask the students which tense they think is being used here. Explain that it is called the past continuous and uses the past tense of the auxiliary verb *to be* in front of the present participle.
- With the class, conjugate the verb *to be* in the simple past (*I was, you were, he/she/it was, we were, you were, they were*), doing the pronoun actions. Underline *was* in **I was** *walking to school* in red on the board.
- Now conjugate the verb *to walk* in the past continuous (*I was walking, you were walking, he/she/it was walking, we were walking, you were walking, they were walking*). Underline *walking* in red on the board, so both parts of the verb (*was walking*) are now underlined in red.
- Look at the two sentences on the board again. Explain that the **simple past** describes an action

that happened in the past, which started and finished within a specific time (e.g. *I walked to school today*).
- The **past continuous** describes an action that had started and was still happening in the past (e.g. *I was walking to school when we met*).

Activity Page
- The students conjugate the verb *to be* in the simple past tense.
- Next they read the sentences, underlining the verbs in red and the pronouns in pink, before rewriting the sentences in the past continuous.
- Finally, they read the sentences at the bottom of the page and join each one to the correct tense.

Extension Activity
- Write the following sentences on the board:
  1. *The centipede was munching a tasty leaf.*
  2. *The centipede munches a tasty leaf.*
  3. *The centipede is munching a tasty leaf.*
  4. *The centipede munched a tasty leaf.*
- The students read each sentence and decide which tense it is in.

Finishing the Lesson
- Read through the page with the students and check their answers.

Spelling: Soft ⟨g⟩

Spelling Test
- The students turn to the backs of their books and find the column labeled *Spelling Test 9*.
- In any order, call out the spelling words learned last week. The students write the words on the lines.

Review
- Use the "vowel hand" (see page 24) to review the five vowel letters and their short and long sounds.
- Review the main alternative spellings for the long vowel sounds using flash cards.
- Then review the soft ⟨c⟩ spelling, and the /ng/ sound and its spellings: ⟨ng⟩ as in *long, strength,* and *singing,* and ⟨n⟩ as in *drink, extinct,* and *anger.*

Spelling Point
- Review the soft ⟨g⟩ spelling. Remind the class that when the letter ⟨g⟩ is followed by ⟨e⟩, ⟨i⟩, or ⟨y⟩, it usually makes the /j/ sound (e.g. *large, magic, gym*).
- Write ⟨ge⟩, ⟨gi⟩, and ⟨gy⟩ on the board and ask the students to call out as many soft ⟨g⟩ words as they can. Make a list of words for each spelling and identify the soft ⟨g⟩ in each word with the class.

Spelling List
- Read the spelling words with the students and identify the soft ⟨g⟩ in each one.
- Ask the class to highlight the ⟨ge⟩, ⟨gi⟩, or ⟨gy⟩ making the /j/ sound.
- Explain the meanings of any unfamiliar words.
- Explain that sometimes the ⟨e⟩ in ⟨ge⟩ is doing two things at once: it is part of the soft ⟨g⟩ spelling, and it is also a "magic ⟨e⟩," making the short vowel in front of the ⟨g⟩ into a long one (e.g. *page, stage*). However, in words of more than one syllable the long vowel tends to get swallowed and sounds more like /ij/ (e.g. *cabbage, luggage*).
- Point out that in words like *gender, margin,* and *gymnastics,* the ⟨e⟩, ⟨i⟩, and ⟨y⟩ each says its own sound, as well as helping to make the /j/ sound.
- It may help the students to remember which alternative spelling to use if the words are put together in a silly sentence: for example, *The strange giraffe did angelic gymnastics on a magical stage.*
- It is a good idea to blend and sound out the spelling words quickly every day with the students.

Spelling List
page
margin
angel
digital
germ
stage
giraffe
engine
change
magical
strange
energy
gender
genetic
gymnastics
emergency
dungeon
urgency

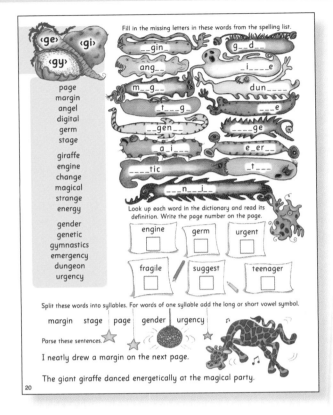

Activity Page
- The students complete the words from the spelling list (in the germs) by writing in the missing letters.
- Next, the students use a dictionary to look up the words in the pages. They read each definition and write the page numbers in the boxes.
- Then they identify the vowel sounds in the words and separate the words into syllables (*mar/gin, gen/der, ur/gen/cy*). *Stage* and *page* are monosyllabic, so the students add the long vowel mark.
- Finally, the students parse the sentences, underlining each part of speech in the correct color.
  I neatly drew a margin on the next page.
  The giant giraffe danced energetically at the magical party.

Dictation
- Provide a sheet of paper for each student and dictate the following sentences:

  1. The large gem was a logical choice.
  2. There was a page on giant orange vegetables.
  3. It was urgent they were told of the danger.

Extension Activity
- The students make a list of words for each of the soft ⟨g⟩ spellings: ⟨ge⟩, ⟨gi⟩, ⟨gy⟩.

Grammar: Places as Proper Nouns

Aim
- Develop the students' ability to identify place names as proper nouns, which always start with a capital letter.

Introduction
- Remind the students that nouns can be divided into **proper nouns** and **common nouns**.
- Proper nouns start with a capital letter and are the names given to particular people, places, and dates.
- Call out some nouns. Ask the students to decide whether they are common nouns or proper nouns, and do the appropriate action (see page 6 of this *Teacher's Book*).
- Ask the students to think of examples of proper nouns. Ask one student to come and write his or her proper noun on the board. Check that the student has started the word with a capital letter.

Main Point
- So far, the main focus for proper nouns has been on people's names and dates (particularly the spelling and sequence of the days of the week and the months of the year). It is important that the students can also identify place names as proper nouns and that they know to start them with a capital letter.
- Ask the students to suggest some places they know: for example, important buildings and monuments, road names, cities, districts (e.g. counties, states, and provinces), and countries. The places could be famous (e.g. the Eiffel Tower in Paris and the Sydney Opera House in Australia) or local (the students could look at leaflets for local attractions and at local maps to find examples).
- Now see if the students know the names of the continents (Africa, Antarctica, Asia, Australasia, Europe, North America, and South America). Ask them which continent they live on (they could look in an atlas or find the simple world map on page 14 of the *Jolly Dictionary*).
- The students could also look at a diagram of the Solar System and find the names of the planets.
- Sometimes, proper nouns have more than one word, particularly monuments (e.g. the Statue of Liberty), buildings (e.g. the Leaning Tower of Pisa), and book titles (e.g. *The Enormous Turnip*).
- Explain that these proper nouns do not need a capital letter at the beginning of every word; only the really important words have a capital letter, not the small joining words (e.g. *the, and, of*). However, it is important to note that book titles always use a capital letter for the first word, even if it is a small word like *the*.

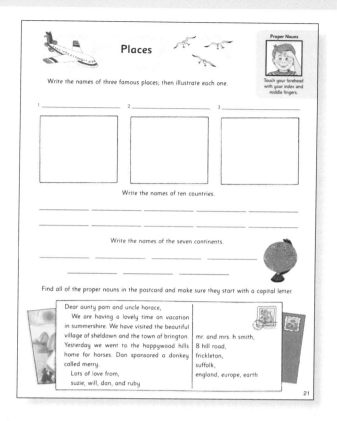

Activity Page
- The students write the names of three famous places and illustrate each one underneath. The places could be local, in the same country, or abroad.
- Using an atlas, the students find and write down the names of ten countries, and then the names of the seven continents.
- Finally, they read the postcard and identify all of the proper nouns, underlining them in black. Using a colored pen or pencil, they add in the capital letters, where appropriate.

Extension Activity
- The students design a poster or postcard for a local attraction, a vacation destination, or for their school.
- Make sure that the name of the place is easy to see and has the correct capital letters. The posters or postcards could then be made into a display.
- Alternatively, the students could label the continents on an outline world map and then color it in.

Finishing the Lesson
- Read through the page with the students and check their answers.

Spelling: The ‹tch› Spelling of the /ch/ Sound

Spelling Test
- The students turn to the backs of their books and find the column labeled *Spelling Test 10*.
- In any order, call out the spelling words learned last week. The students write the words on the lines.

Review
- Review the soft ‹c› and soft ‹g› spellings, and the ‹n› spelling of the /ng/ sound, as in *drink, extinct,* and *anger.*
- Write the following words on the board: *dance, city, face, giant, magic, large, anger, drank, anchor.*
- Blend and sound out the words with the class, and identify the different spelling patterns.

Spelling Point
- Introduce the ‹tch› spelling of the /ch/ sound. This spelling usually follows a single vowel letter saying a short vowel sound: ‹-atch›, ‹-etch›, ‹-itch›, ‹-otch›, ‹-utch› (as in *match, fetch, itch, hopscotch, hutch*). The main exceptions are *rich, such, much, which, attach,* and *sandwich.*
- Write some ‹tch› words on the board. Blend and sound them out with the class, and identify the short vowel in front of each ‹tch›.

Spelling List
- Read the spelling words with the students and identify the short vowel followed by ‹tch› in each one.
- Ask the class to highlight the ‹tch›.
- Explain the meanings of any unfamiliar words.
- Point out the ‹u› spelling of the little /oo/ in *butcher* (acting like a short vowel), the silent ‹w› in *wretched,* and the ‹wa› spelling for /wo/ in *watching.* Remind the students that the plural word *crutches* has the ‹es› spelling because the root word ends in ‹ch›.
- Write *witch* and *which* on the board and ask the students for their different meanings. Remind them that words that sound the same but have different spellings and meanings are called *homophones.*
- Tell the class to draw a small pointed hat over the ‹t› in *witch* to help them remember which one it is.
- It will help the students know when to use the ‹tch› spelling if they remember that it usually comes after a single vowel letter saying a short vowel sound.

itch
catch
fetch
witch
match
hutch
kitchen
snatch
butcher
switch
sketch
crutches
watching
stretcher
ketchup
wretched
scratching
stretching

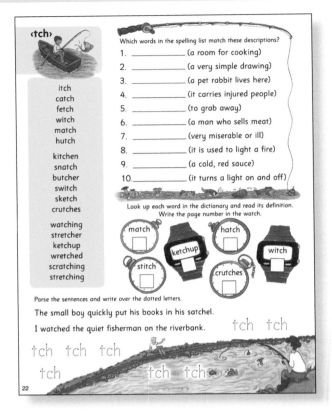

Activity Page
- The students read the phrases and decide which words from the spelling list they describe.
- Next, they use a dictionary to look up the words in the watches. They read each definition and write the page numbers in the boxes.
- The students parse the sentences, underlining each part of speech in the correct color.
  The small boy quickly put his books in his satchel.
  I watched the quiet fisherman on the riverbank.
- Finally, they write over the dotted letters, ‹tch›.

Dictation
- Provide a sheet of paper for each student and dictate the following sentences:

1. I went to the kitchen to fetch the ketchup.
2. We watched the butcher cut up the meat.
3. He stretched his arms and legs when he stood up.

Extension Activity
- The students draw a picture of a rabbit hutch in their Spelling Word Books. Inside the hutch they list as many ‹tch› words they can.

Grammar: Proper Adjectives

Aim
• Refine the students' knowledge of adjectives, and develop their ability to identify proper adjectives in sentences.

Introduction
• Review proper nouns. Ask the students to suggest some proper nouns and write them on the board. Write them without a capital letter and see whether the class notices.
• Remind the students that proper nouns are the names given to particular people, places, and dates and, because they are special, they need a capital letter.
• Review adjectives and the action for them (touch the side of your temple with your fist).
• Remind the students that adjectives are words that describe nouns (or pronouns) and the color for them is blue.
• Call out a noun and ask the students to think of adjectives to describe it.

Main Point
• Tell the students that some adjectives are proper adjectives, just as some nouns are proper nouns. In fact, proper adjectives come from proper nouns, so they always start with a capital letter. Most proper adjectives describe something in terms of nationality, religion, or culture.
• Ask the students what country they live in, and what word is used to describe the people, places, and things in that country.
• Write some countries on the board and ask the students if they know the proper adjectives for them (e.g. America/American, Australia/Australian, Britain/British, Canada/Canadian, Egypt/Egyptian, India/Indian, Nigeria/Nigerian, Scotland/Scottish, Thailand/Thai, Wales/Welsh).
• Many proper adjectives end with ‹-ish›, ‹-ese›, ‹-ian›, or ‹-an›. Write these suffixes on the board, leaving room for an extra column at the end, and see how many proper adjectives the students can suggest for each one. If they find it difficult, call out some countries and ask the students if they know the proper adjectives for them.
- ‹-ish›: *British, English, Irish, Polish, Scottish, Spanish, Swedish*
- ‹-ese›: *Chinese, Japanese, Vietnamese, Nepalese*
- ‹-ian›: *Australian, Canadian, Egyptian, Indian, Italian, Nigerian, Peruvian*
- ‹-an›: *American, German, Kenyan, Korean, Mexican*
• Some proper adjectives do not follow a pattern.

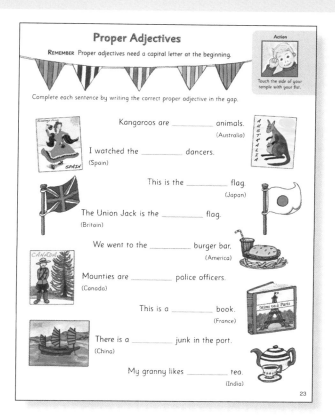

Think of some examples with the class, and write them in the last column (examples include *French, Greek, Thai, Welsh*).
• Tell the class that there are proper adjectives for the continents too.
• Ask the students to name the continents, and see if they know the proper adjectives for them. Then write them on the board (*Europe/European, Africa/African, Australasia/Australasian, North America/North American, South America/South American, Antarctica/Antarctic*).

Activity Page
• The students read each sentence (and the country name in brackets). Then they decide which proper adjective fits in the gap and write it on the line.

Extension Activity
• Write the following countries and proper adjectives on the board:
Wales, Ireland, Nigeria, Thailand, Australia, Peru, Japan, India, Sweden, Great Britain, Egypt;
Nigerian, Welsh, Japanese, Thai, Irish, Peruvian, Australian, British, Indian, Swedish, Egyptian.
• The students write them down in pairs.
• Alternatively, write the countries and proper adjectives onto small pieces of card and place them on a table so that the students can play "pairs."

Spelling: *The ‹dge› Spelling of the /j/ Sound*

Spelling Test

- The students turn to the backs of their books and find the column labeled *Spelling Test 11*.
- In any order, call out the spelling words learned last week. The students write the words on the lines.

Review

- Review the soft ‹c›, soft ‹g›, and ‹tch› spellings, and the ‹n› spelling of the /ng/ sound, as in *drink, extinct*, and *anger*.
- Write the following words on the board: *circle, poli**ce**, twi**ce**, dan**g**er, oran**g**e, **g**erm, ha**tch**, sni**tch**, an**g**ler, blanket, skunk*.
- Blend and sound out the words with the class, identifying the different spelling patterns.

Spelling Point

- Introduce the ‹dge› spelling of the /j/ sound. This spelling is usually used after a single vowel letter saying a short vowel sound: ‹-adge›, ‹-edge›, ‹-idge›, ‹-odge›, ‹-udge› (as in *badge, hedge, ridge, dodge, fudge*).
- Write some ‹dge› words on the board. Blend and sound them out with the class, and identify the short vowel in front of each ‹dge›.

Spelling List

edge
judge
sledge
badge
badger
bridge
gadget
budge
fidget
ledge
hedgerow
hedgehog
knowledge
begrudge
porridge
budgerigar
drawbridge
partridge

- Read the spelling words with the students and identify the short vowel followed by ‹dge› in each one. Ask the class to highlight the ‹dge›.
- Explain the meanings of any unfamiliar words.
- Point out the different spellings of the /j/ sound in *judge*, the ‹ow› spelling in *hedgerow*, and the silent ‹k› in *knowledge*.
- It will help the students know when to use the ‹dge› spelling if they remember that it usually comes after a single vowel letter saying a short vowel sound.
- It may also help the students to remember which spelling to use if the words are put together in a silly sentence: for example, *The partridge had to budge from his ledge as the badgers and hedgehogs edged past the hedge with their porridge.*

Activity Page

- The students write ‹dge› on the line to complete each word.

- They illustrate each word in the box.
- Next, they use a dictionary to look up the words in the hedgehogs. They read each definition and write the page numbers in the boxes.
- At the bottom of the page, they write over the dotted letters, ‹dge›.
- Finally, the students parse the sentences, underlining each part of speech in the correct color. Remind them that the first sentence is written in the present continuous so the auxiliary verb (*are*) needs to be underlined in red as well as the main verb (*waiting*).
  We are waiting eagerly for the judge.
  The badger quickly disappeared through the hedge.

Dictation

- Provide a sheet of paper for each student and dictate the following sentences:

1. We had fun in the snow playing on our sledge.
2. I saw a hedgehog hiding under the hedge.
3. The sledgehammer was very big and heavy.

Extension Activity

- The students draw a picture of a hedgehog in their Spelling Word Books. Inside the hedgehog they list as many ‹dge› words they can.

Grammar: *More Syllables*

Aim
• Develop the students' ability to separate words into syllables.

Introduction
• Remind the students that words are made up of units of sound called syllables and that each syllable has one vowel sound.
• Write these words on the board: *request, hedgehog, germ, bluebell, princess, unimportant*.
• Identify the vowel sounds with the class and underline them on the board.
• Finally, separate the words into syllables with a line (*re/quest, hedge/hog, germ, blue/bell, prin/cess, un/im/por/tant*).
• Say the words with the class, clapping once for every syllable. Stress each vowel sound, especially if it is a schwa (a swallowed vowel sound), as this can help reinforce the spelling.

Main Point
• Explain that breaking down words into syllables can help make spelling easier, especially for longer words. The students will find that doing this aurally becomes quite easy with practice. However, when the students are asked to separate words into syllables with a line, it will help them to know the following simple rules:
• **Double consonants**: write *puppet* on the board and identify the vowel sounds with the students. Now ask the students where they think the line should go to separate the syllables. Explain that when a consonant is doubled in a word, the line goes between them. Draw a line between the two ‹p›s (*pup/pet*) and repeat this activity with other words (e.g. *hap/pen, bit/ten, rot/ten, bat/ted, hum/ming*). Take care with words like *hopped, stopped,* and *nipped*, which have a silent ‹e›. These may look like two-syllable words but they are, in fact, monosyllabic.
• **‹ck› words**: write *pocket* on the board and ask the students where the line separating the syllables should go. The class may say it goes between the ‹c› and ‹k› because the letters make the same sound. However, ‹ck› words are an exception; the line is usually put after the ‹k› (e.g. *pock/et*). Write other words on the board for the students to split into syllables (e.g. *crack/er, rock/et, chick/en, crick/et*).
• **‹le› words**: now write *candle, label,* and *pencil* on the board and encourage the students to clap the syllables (*can/dle, la/bel, pen/cil*). The sounds represented by the ‹le› spelling are the same as those for ‹el› and ‹il› and consist of a small schwa

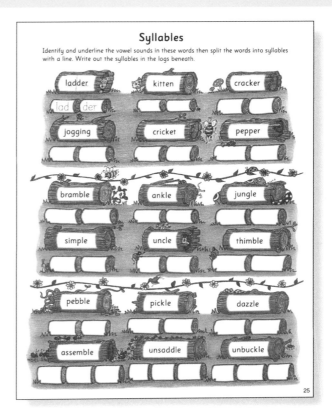

Syllables

Identify and underline the vowel sounds in these words then split the words into syllables with a line. Write out the syllables in the logs beneath.

ladder | kitten | cracker
lad der | |
jogging | cricket | pepper
| |
bramble | ankle | jungle
| |
simple | uncle | thimble
| |
pebble | pickle | dazzle
| |
assemble | unsaddle | unbuckle
| |

25

before the /l/. However, the schwa (a swallowed vowel sound) can clearly be seen in *label* and *pencil* but not in *candle*. In ‹le› words, there is no written vowel to underline in the last syllable. Instead, when the students see a word like this, they must listen for the schwa and draw a line before the consonant preceding it (e.g. *can/dle, sad/dle*). Again, ‹ck› words are an exception; the line usually goes after the ‹k› (e.g. *pick/le, cack/le, buck/le*). Write some more words on the board and split them into syllables (e.g. *ram/ble, an/kle, tem/ple, doo/dle, pick/le, nee/dle*).

Activity Page
• In each section, the students identify the syllables in the words by underlining the vowel sounds and separating them with a line, following the rules outlined above.
• Then they write out the syllables in the smaller logs underneath.

Extension Activity
• Write some three-syllable words on the board and ask the students to separate them into syllables.
• Good examples include: *rec/tan/gle, be/daz/zle, be/lit/tle, blue/bot/tle, un/sup/ple, ca/boo/dle, em/bat/tle, en/tan/gle, re/set/tle, re/kin/dle*.

Spelling: ‹le›

Spelling Test
- The students turn to the backs of their books and find the column labeled *Spelling Test 12*.
- In any order, call out the spelling words learned last week. The students write the words on the lines.

Review
- Review the soft ‹c›, soft ‹g›, ‹tch›, and ‹dge› spellings, and the ‹n› spelling of the /ng/ sound, as in *drink, extinct,* and *anger.*
- Write the following words on the board: *ra**ce**, ri**ce**, **c**ymbal, an**g**el, gin**g**er, **g**ym, i**tch**, e**dge**, dri**n**k, exti**n**ct.* Blend and sound out the words with the class, and identify the different spelling patterns.

Spelling Point
- Review the ‹le› spelling. Remind the class that this spelling comes at the end of multisyllabic words, and sounds something like /ool/.
- This vowel sound, which is swallowed, is known as a *schwa.* Like other vowels, the schwa can influence a short stressed vowel in the previous syllable, so the consonant doubling rule applies, as in words like *apple* and *little.* No doubling rule is necessary in words like *ankle, jingle,* and *bundle* because they already have two consonants between the short vowel and the ‹le› (see page 24).
- Write some ‹le› words on the board, and blend and sound them out with the class.

Spelling List
- Read the spelling words with the students and identify the ‹le› spelling in each one. Ask the class to highlight the ‹le›, and underline any double consonants (e.g. the ‹zz› in *puzzle*).
- Explain the meanings of any unfamiliar words.
- Point out the different spellings of the /ee/ sound in *eagle* and *beetle,* the ‹n› as /ng/ spelling in *angle, jungle,* and *rectangle,* the silent ‹k› in *knuckle,* the ‹ie› in *believable,* and the ‹h› in *vehicle* (the students could say /vee-hic-le/ to help them remember the spelling).
- It may also help the students to remember which spelling to use if the words are put together in a silly sentence: for example, *The jungle proved to be a formidable obstacle for the simple vehicle.*

| simple |
| eagle |
| beetle |
| handle |
| puzzle |
| angle |
| jungle |
| horrible |
| terrible |
| knuckle |
| disable |
| obstacle |
| formidable |
| improbable |
| impossible |
| rectangle |
| believable |
| vehicle |

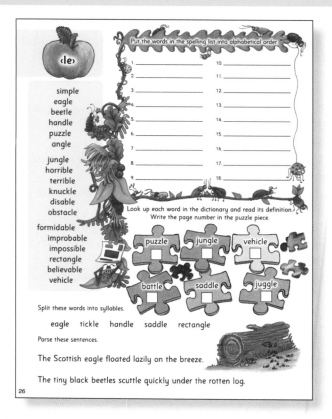

Activity Page
- The students put the words from the spelling list into alphabetical order (*angle, beetle, believable, disable, eagle, formidable, handle, horrible, impossible, improbable, jungle, knuckle, obstacle, puzzle, rectangle, simple, terrible, vehicle*).
- Next, they use a dictionary to look up the words in the puzzle pieces. They read each definition and write the page numbers in the boxes. The students could also write down the meanings for some of these words.
- Then they identify the vowel sounds in the words and separate the words into syllables (*ea/gle, tick/le, han/dle, sad/dle, rec/tan/gle*).
- Finally, the students parse the sentences, underlining each part of speech in the correct color.
  The Scottish eagle floated lazily on the breeze.
  The tiny black beetles scuttle quickly under the rotten log.

Dictation
- Provide a sheet of paper for each student and dictate the following sentences:

  1. The kettle was boiling on the fire.
  2. My uncle has a stable for his horse.
  3. There was an apple in the middle of the table.

Grammar: Paragraphs *(Organizing Information)*

Aim
- Develop the students' understanding of paragraphs and teach them how to use them to organize their writing.

Introduction
- Show the class a block of text that fills the page and is not organized into paragraphs. Now show the class an example of a reading book page where there are several paragraphs to look at. (In both cases, the students do not need to be able to read the words, but they should be able to see the layout clearly.)
- Ask them what they notice about the shape of the writing and which page they would prefer to read. The students are more likely to prefer the reading book layout because the text is broken down into smaller sections, which are easier to read.

Main Point
- Explain that these small blocks of writing are called paragraphs. A new paragraph starts on a new line, making a long piece of writing easier to read. Paragraphs are also a way of organizing information so it is easier to understand. A paragraph is a group of sentences that are put together because they describe one idea or topic. By putting paragraphs in a particular order, a piece of writing can move from one idea to another in a way that makes sense.
- Tell the students they are going to do a piece of writing about themselves. First of all, they need to think about what they would like to say. Then they can think about how they might organize their ideas into paragraphs.
- Ask the students which topics they would like to write about. It might help to start them off with topics such as *me and my family, where I live, my hobbies, my friends, my school, my pets.*
- Write these topic headings on the board, along with some of their suggestions, leaving some space for more information. Tell the students that these are the headings for their paragraphs.
- Now suggest some ideas that could go in the paragraphs, for example, *my favorite lessons, my friends' names, my teachers.* Ask the students which heading each idea should go under; *my favorite lessons* and *my teachers* could go under the heading *my school,* for example.
- Other possible ideas include the following: *what I look like, the sports I play, why I like my friends, the pets I have, my home, the clubs I belong to, the people in my family, my garden, the music I like, what I do at school, the clothes I wear, time*

with my friends, what my pets eat, my bedroom.
- Ask the students for more ideas. Discuss where each one should go and add them to the board.

Activity Page
- The students draw a picture of themselves in the middle of the page.
- Next, they trace over the paragraph headings in the first three clouds.
- In the fourth cloud, the students choose a fourth topic heading from the board and copy it onto the first line.
- They decide which ideas they want to put underneath each heading and write their ideas on the lines.

Extension Activity
- The students think of more ideas for each topic and add them to the clouds.

Finishing the Lesson
- Call out a heading and ask some of the students to read out the ideas they put under it.
- Look at the page with the students, checking that their ideas are organized underneath appropriate headings.

Spelling: ‹qu›

Spelling Test
- The students turn to the backs of their books and find the column labeled *Spelling Test 13.*
- In any order, call out the spelling words learned last week. The students write the words on the lines.

Review
- Review the soft ‹c›, soft ‹g›, ‹tch›, ‹dge›, and ‹le› spellings, and the ‹n› spelling of the /ng/ sound, as in *drink, extinct,* and *anger.*
- Write the following words on the board: *space, margin, hatch, snitch, badge, lodge, apple, kettle, anger, skunk.*
- Blend and sound out the words with the class, and identify the different spelling patterns.

Spelling Point
- Review the ‹qu› spelling of the /qu/ sound. Remind the class that /qu/ is really two sounds, /k/ and /w/, blended together. When the students hear /kw/ in a word, they must remember to write ‹qu›.
- Explain that the letter ‹q› is always followed by a ‹u› in English words.
- Ask the students to suggest some words with the ‹qu› spelling. write them on the board and blend and sound them out with the class.

Spelling List
- Read the spelling words with the students and identify the ‹qu› spelling in each one. Ask the class to highlight the ‹qu›.
- Explain the meanings of any unfamiliar words.
- Point out the ‹el› spelling in *quarrel* and *squirrel*, comparing it with the ‹le› spelling of words like *beetle* and *jungle.*
- It is a good idea to blend and sound out the spelling words quickly every day with the students. Emphasize the /el/ in *quarrel* and *squirrel* and the /or/ in *equator* to help the students with their spelling.

quiver
equal
request
quote
liquid
squeak
quite
quarrel
squeeze
squirrel
squash
aquatic
conquest
banquet
aquarium
equipment
eloquent
equator

Activity Page
- The students read the phrases and decide which words from the spelling list they describe.
- Next, they use a dictionary to look up the words in the squares. They read each definition and write the page numbers in the boxes. The students could also write down the meanings for some of these words.

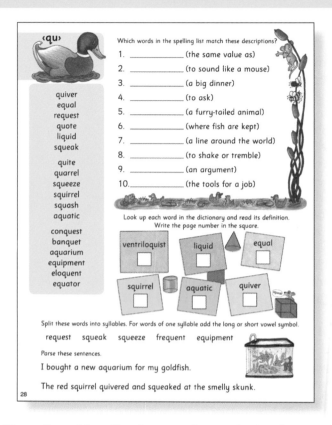

- Then they identify the vowel sounds in the words and separate the words into syllables (*re/quest, fre/quent, e/quip/ment*). *Squeak* and *squeeze* are monosyllabic, so the students add the long vowel mark instead. It is important to remember that it is the vowel sounds in a word that determine the number of syllables, not the number of vowel letters.
- Finally, the students parse the sentences, underlining each part of speech in the correct color.

I bought a new aquarium for my goldfish.

The red squirrel quivered and squeaked at the smelly skunk.

Dictation
- Provide a sheet of paper for each student and dictate the sentences below. Remind the students that *Queen Nooka* in the first sentence, and *Class Two* in the second are proper nouns and need capital letters.

1. Queen Nooka quickly caught the bunch of flowers.
2. Class Two won the table quiz.
3. An archer keeps arrows in a quiver.

Extension Activity
- The students draw a picture of a duck in their Spelling Word Books. Inside the duck they list as many ‹qu› words they can.

Grammar: *Paragraphs* (All About Me)

Aim
• Develop the students' ability to write in a way that is easy to read and understand by using paragraphs.

Introduction
• Remind the students about paragraphs. Paragraphs break down a longer piece of text into smaller sections. Each one starts on a new line and is made up of sentences that describe one idea or topic.
• With the students, look at the cloud pages they worked on in the previous lesson. Discuss the topics and the ideas they put down for each one.

Main Point
• Remind the students that paragraphs are a way of organizing information in a piece of writing so that it is easy to read and understand.
• Before they write anything, it is important that the students think about the different things they want to say and the order in which they should say them, so that their writing makes sense. The students can then expand their ideas into proper sentences and put them together to make paragraphs. Doing this will help their writing flow and be more interesting.
• Ask some of the students to choose a heading and say one or two sentences about it, using the ideas from their cloud page.
• Write some of their sentences on the board and discuss whether the sentences make sense and follow a logical order.
• Remember to encourage the students to use paragraphs in their writing from now on.

Activity Page
• The students use their cloud pages (page 27 of their *Student Books*) to do a piece of writing about themselves, using paragraphs.
• The students trace over the heading *Me and My Family* at the top of the page.
• Encourage the students to think about how they will use their notes from the cloud page to write some sentences about themselves and their families.
• Remind the students that a paragraph always starts on a new line and explain that the first line is usually indented.
• *Indented* means that the sentence starts a little way in from the edge of the paper. Point out that the first line of each paragraph on their *Student Book* page starts a little further in than the rest of the lines.
• Encourage the students to indent the first line of their paragraphs from now on.

Paragraphs
Write over each heading.
Then write a paragraph about that topic underneath.

All About Me

Me and My Family

Where I Live

My Hobbies

29

• Sometimes in printed text the paragraph is not indented; instead, there is a line space between the end of one paragraph and the beginning of the next.
• Ask the students what their first sentence might be. Remind them to add as many interesting details as they can.
• The students trace over the remaining headings on their *Student Book* page.
• They write a few sentences underneath each heading to make their paragraphs.

Extension Activity
• Provide some lined paper for each student.
• The students write a paragraph for the fourth heading on their cloud page.
• Alternatively, they could think of a topic heading of their own and write a paragraph about it.

Finishing the Lesson
• Ask some of the students to read one of their paragraphs aloud.
• If anything seems out of place or in the wrong order, discuss how it could be improved with the class.

Spelling: The ‹s› Spelling of the /z/ Sound

Spelling Test
- The students turn to the backs of their books and find the column labeled *Spelling Test 14*.
- In any order, call out the spelling words learned last week. The students write the words on the lines.

Review
- Review the soft ‹c›, soft ‹g›, ‹tch›, ‹dge›, ‹le›, and ‹qu› spellings, and the ‹n› spelling of the /ng/ sound, as in *drink, extinct,* and *anger.*
- Write the following words on the board: *twice, page, fetch, bridge, simple, puzzle, quiver, question, junk, defunct.* Blend and sound out the words with the class, and identify the different spelling patterns.

Spelling Point
- Initially, the students are taught that the /z/ sound is made by the letter ‹z›.
- However, many common words with the /z/ sound are written with the letter ‹s› (e.g. *goes, does, is, rose, as*). So, the students already know that sometimes the letter ‹s› makes the /z/ sound.
- When blending, the students can use the rule "if one way doesn't work, try the other" to read these words, but for correct spelling, the words will need to be learned.

Spelling List
- Read the spelling words with the students and identify the ‹s› making the /z/ sound in each one. Ask the class to highlight the ‹s›.
- Explain the meanings of any unfamiliar words.
- Point out the ‹u› spelling of the /i/ sound in *busy* and *business*, the ‹ph› in *phase*, and the silent ‹e› on the end of *inquisitive*. Emphasize the /p/ in *raspberry* and the /i/ in *business*, and say */en-thus-I-astic/* to help the students with their spelling.
- It may help the students remember the ‹s› spelling of the /z/ sound if they put together a silly sentence, using as many of the words as possible.
- It is a good idea to blend and sound out the spelling words quickly every day.

easy
busy
nose
result
prison
dismal
cosmic
positive
misery
present
president
raspberry
phase
invisible
business
inquisitive
preposition
enthusiastic

Activity Page
- The students find the words from the spelling list in the word search and work out which word is missing (*misery*).

Find the words from the spelling list. Which one is missing?

easy
busy
nose
result
prison
dismal

cosmic
positive
misery
present
president
raspberry

phase
invisible
business
inquisitive
preposition
enthusiastic

Look up each word in the dictionary and read its definition. Write the page number in the daisy.

desert   easel   laser
noodles   marbles   raisin

Split these words into syllables. For words of one syllable add the long or short vowel symbol.

dismal   nose   clumsy   drowsy   raspberry

Parse these sentences.

I carefully cut the paper with my sharp scissors.

He quickly ate the English raspberries and cream for dessert.

30

- Next, they use a dictionary to look up the words in the daisies. They read each definition and write the page numbers in the boxes. The students could also write down the meanings for some of these words.
- Then they identify the vowel sounds in the words and separate the words into syllables (*dis/mal, clum/sy, drow/sy, rasp/ber/ry*). *Nose* only has one syllable, so the students add the long vowel mark instead.
- Finally, the students parse the sentences, underlining each part of speech in the correct color. Remind them that *my* is a possessive adjective used to describe who the scissors belong to, and that *English* is a proper adjective, which needs a capital letter.

I carefully cut the paper with my sharp scissors.
He quickly ate the English raspberries and cream for dessert.

Dictation
- Provide a sheet of paper for each student and dictate the following sentences:

1. We reserved some seats for two concerts.
2. We played marbles indoors as it was raining.
3. The weasel had measles.

Grammar: Speech Marks

Aim
- Develop the students' understanding of speech marks and encourage them to use speech marks in their writing.

Introduction
- Draw a rough picture of a person on the board (or put up a picture from a magazine) and add a speech bubble coming out of the person's mouth.
- Ask the students what the speech bubble is for. Then ask them what they think the person is saying and write one of their suggestions inside.
- With the students, discuss where something like this might be found (e.g. in comic books and certain story books).
- Now ask them what happens when you want to put speech in a piece of writing. How do we know which bits are speech and which are not?
- Remind the class about speech marks and how to use them. It may help the students remember how to write them correctly if they think of speech marks as a "66" before the speech and as a "99" after it.
- Say the sentence from the speech bubble aloud and act out the punctuation. (Hold up one hand and bend the index and middle finger up and down to represent the opening speech marks. Then say the sentence and draw the comma with a finger on the other hand. Next, hold that hand up and bend the index and middle finger up and down for the closing speech marks. Finally, say *said Sam*, for example, and point with a finger to make the period.) Remember to do this in "mirror" writing when facing the students. Encourage the students to act out the punctuation with you.
- Remind the students that they do not have to use the word *said* every time. Encourage them to use other words (e.g. *shouted, whispered, groaned, cried*).

Main Point
- Now write the sentence on the board, using speech marks. As you write, explain what you are doing. Tell the students to start with "66," then write what the person says, remembering to start with a capital letter. When they have finished writing the speech, they put a comma at the end, before closing with "99." They must remember to say who is speaking and end with a period.
- Try to avoid questions or exclamations for now as they need a question or exclamation mark rather than a comma. Question marks and exclamation marks in speech will be introduced later on in the *Grammar 3 Student Book*.

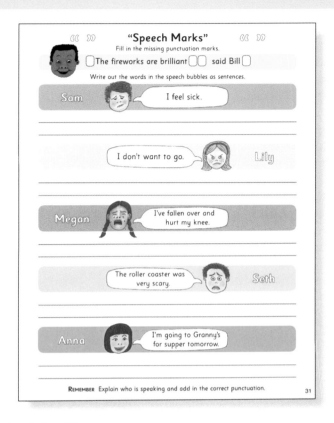

Activity Page
- The students write in the outlined speech marks at the top of the page. Then they fill in the missing punctuation marks in the first sentence.
- Lastly, they write out the words in the speech bubbles as sentences, explaining who is speaking and using the correct punctuation.

Extension Activity
- Provide some lined paper and old magazines or comic books for the students. The students cut out pictures of people or cartoon characters from the magazines.
- They each glue one of the pictures to a sheet of paper and draw a speech bubble coming from the mouth. Then they add some speech to their speech bubble and write the speech out in a sentence underneath, using speech marks.

Finishing the Lesson
- Write one of the sentences on the board without any punctuation. Ask one of the students to come up and put in the punctuation.
- Erase the word *said* and ask whether anyone used another word instead. Ask for more suggestions, writing in the new word each time.
- Remind the students to use speech marks as well as paragraphs in their writing from now on.

Spelling: ‹se› and ‹ze› Making the /z/ Sound

Spelling Test
- The students turn to the backs of their books and find the column labeled *Spelling Test 15*.
- In any order, call out the spelling words learned last week. The students write the words on the lines.

Review
- Review the soft ‹c›, soft ‹g›, ‹tch›, ‹dge›, ‹le›, and ‹qu› spellings, the ‹n› spelling of the /ng/ sound, as in *drink, extinct,* and *anger,* and the ‹s› spelling of /z/.
- Write the following words on the board: *can**c**el, ge**rm**, hu**tch**, ju**dge**, ea**g**le, e**q**ual, trun**k**, an**ch**or, ea**s**y, mea**s**les.* Blend and sound out the words with the class, and identify the different spelling patterns.

Spelling Point
- Remind the students that they know two ways to write the /z/ sound, and ask them what they are (the ‹z› and ‹s› spellings). Then tell them that there are another two ways to write it, which are ‹se› and ‹ze›.
- Write the words *sneeze* and *noise* on the board, identify the ‹ze› and ‹se› spellings, and explain that they usually come at the end of a word. Point out that the ‹e› in both words is a "silent ‹e›."
- Now write the words *chose* and *prize* on the board. Point out that these are not the same as the first two words. The ‹e› in both words is part of a "hop-over ‹e›" digraph: ‹o_e› and ‹i_e›. This makes them examples of the ‹s› and ‹z› spellings of /z/.

Spelling List
- Read the spelling words with the students and identify the ‹se› or ‹ze› making the /z/ sound in each one. Ask the class to highlight the letters making the /z/ sound.
- Explain the meanings of any unfamiliar words.
- Point out the ‹au› spelling in *pause, cause,* and *applause,* the ‹ow› in *browse,* the ‹ui› in *bruise,* the ‹ur› and ‹qu› in *turquoise,* and the two different spellings of the /ai/ sound in *mayonnaise.*
- It may help the students remember the ‹se› and ‹ze› spellings if they put together a silly sentence, using as many of the words as possible.

ooze
sneeze
cheese
choose
freeze
wheeze
breeze
noise
browse
bronze
pause
cause
disease
bruise
applause
appraise
turquoise
mayonnaise

Activity Page
- The students put the words from the spelling list into alphabetical order (*applause, appraise, breeze,*

bronze, browse, bruise, cause, cheese, choose, disease, freeze, mayonnaise, noise, ooze, pause, sneeze, turquoise, wheeze). Next, they use a dictionary to look up the words in the cheeses. They read each definition and write the page numbers in the boxes.
- Then they identify the vowel sounds in the words and separate the words into syllables (*ap/praise, tur/quoise, may/on/naise*). *Wheeze* and *please* are monosyllabic, so the students add the long vowel mark instead. Lastly, they parse the sentences, underlining each part of speech in the correct color. Remind them that *American* is a proper adjective, which needs a capital letter, and *our* is a possessive adjective used to describe who the house belongs to.

I sneeze and wheeze in the winter.

The old American jeep reversed noisily outside our house.

Dictation
- Dictate the sentences below. Remind the students that they need to use speech marks, with the correct punctuation, and a capital letter for the proper noun *Anna* in the first sentence. Point out that the third sentence needs a question mark.

1. "Pollen makes me wheeze and sneeze," said Anna.
2. The new bronze statue caused much applause.
3. Can I have cheese on toast please?

Grammar: Speech Marks

Aim
- Refine the students' understanding of speech marks and develop their ability to use them in writing.

Introduction
- Point out the picture of two boys playing ball at the top of their *Student Book* page.
- Discuss the picture with the class (think of names for the boys, decide where they are, and suggest why they are playing ball, and so on).
- Ask the students what one of the boys might be saying and write one of their suggestions on the board in a large speech bubble. Try to avoid questions or exclamations for now as they need a question or exclamation mark at the end of the speech rather than a comma.
- Tell the students they are going to write the speech in a sentence together. Ask them how they would start, and write opening speech marks ("66") on the board. Add the words from the speech bubble, reminding the students to start with a capital letter.
- Ask the students how they show that the speech is finished: write the comma, followed by closing speech marks ("99"). Now ask them what the boy's name is (e.g. Sam) and write *said Sam* at the end.
- Remind the students that names are proper nouns and need a capital letter.
- Encourage the class to think of different words for *said* and write them on the board.
- Say the sentence aloud, acting out the punctuation (see page 61), and encourage the students to join in.

Main Point
- Look at the picture again, and discuss what the second boy might be saying. Write one of the suggestions in a big speech bubble, as before.
- Tell the students they are going to write the rest of the conversation in a sentence, but this time they will start with the boy's name (e.g. Ben).
- Write *Ben replied* on a new line underneath the first sentence. Explain that when a new person starts speaking, the students have to start on a new line. This makes it clear to the reader that a different person is speaking.
- Remind the students that when they write the speech this way around, the comma comes after *replied* and does not go inside the speech marks. Add the comma and write the speech, opening with "66" speech marks and closing with "99" speech marks.
- Remind the class to use a capital letter at the beginning of the speech and a period at the end.
- Avoid exclamations or questions for now.

Activity Page
- The students write what the boys are saying in the speech bubbles. They can either use the sentences from the board or make up their own.
- Next, the students write down the boys' conversation in sentences underneath. Encourage them to set the scene by writing something first (e.g. *Sam and Ben are playing in the park...* or *Bill and Jim were getting ready for the big game...*).
- Remind them to start on a new line whenever someone new starts speaking.

Extension Activity
- The students cut out pictures of people or cartoon characters from magazines. They each glue two pictures to a sheet of paper, and draw a speech bubble coming from each mouth.
- Then they look at the two pictures, thinking about what the people might say to each other, and write their words in the speech bubbles.
- Finally, the students write out the speech in sentences, saying who is speaking and using the correct punctuation. Remind them to start a new line when the person who is speaking changes.

Finishing the Lesson
- Ask some of the students to read out their sentences and act out the punctuation.

Spelling: The ‹-less› Suffix

Spelling Test
- The students turn to the backs of their books and find the column labeled *Spelling Test 16*.
- Call out the spelling words learned last week.

Review
- Review the soft ‹c›, soft ‹g›, ‹tch›, ‹dge›, ‹le›, and ‹qu› spellings, the ‹n› spelling of the /ng/ sound, and the ‹s›, ‹se›, and ‹ze› spellings of /z/.
- Write the following words on the board: *office, stage, witch, sledge, beetle, quote, quill, busy, cheese, ooze*. Blend and sound out the words with the class, and identify the different spelling patterns.

Spelling Point
- Review suffixes. Remind the class that a suffix is one or more syllables added at the end of a word to change its meaning. Suffixes can be used to make plural nouns, comparative and superlative adjectives, the simple past tense (e.g. *I walked*), and the present participle (e.g. *walking*).
- Review the spelling rules for adding ‹-ed› and ‹-ing› (see page 25) and add them to the following words on the board: *look* (*looked, looking*), *hop* (*hopped, hopping*), *hope* (*hoped, hoping*), *play* (*played, playing*), *pity* (*pitied, pitying*).
- Now introduce the suffix ‹-less›. This is added to words (usually abstract nouns) to make adjectives. Adjectives ending in ‹-less› describe something as being "without (it)." So, *worthless* means *without worth*, as in *The old clock was worthless*.
- Explain that because ‹-less› starts with a consonant, it is usually just added to the root word, but there is one exception. If a word ends in ‹y› (e.g. *pity*), it is usually because "shy ‹i›" does not like being at the end and has been replaced by "toughy ‹y›." However, if ‹-less› is added (e.g. *pitiless*), "shy ‹i›" returns as it is no longer at the end of the word.

Spelling List
- Read the spelling words with the students and identify the suffix ‹-less› in each one.
- Explain the meanings of any unfamiliar words. Point out the ‹aw› in *flawless*, the ‹or› spelling of /er/ in *worthless*, the ‹are› spelling of /air/ in *careless*, the "shy ‹i›" in *pitiless*, the ‹ea› in *breathless*, the "soft ‹c›" in *priceless*, and the ‹eigh› in *weightless*.

useless
helpless
endless
painless
aimless
flawless
worthless
fearless
timeless
harmless
speechless
bottomless
priceless
careless
pitiless
breathless
flightless
weightless

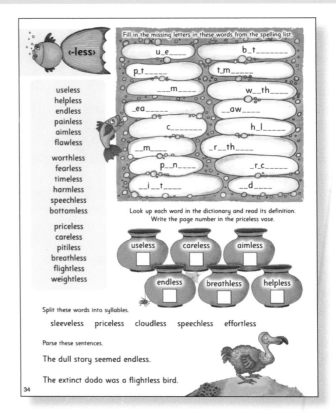

Activity Page
- The students complete the words from the spelling list (in the bubbles) by writing in the missing letters.
- Next, the students use a dictionary to look up the words in the priceless vases. They read each definition and write the page numbers in the boxes. The students could also write down the meanings for some of these words.
- Then they identify the vowel sounds in the words and separate the words into syllables (*sleeve/less, price/less, cloud/less, speech/less, ef/fort/less*).
- Finally, the students parse the sentences, underlining each part of speech in the correct color.
  The <u>dull</u> <u>story</u> <u>seemed</u> <u>endless</u>.
  The <u>extinct</u> <u>dodo</u> <u>was</u> a <u>flightless</u> <u>bird</u>.

Dictation
- Provide a sheet of paper for each student and dictate the sentences below. Point out that *Chinese* is a proper adjective and needs a capital letter. Remind the students to use speech marks with the correct punctuation in the third sentence.

1. That Chinese vase was priceless.
2. The well seemed to be bottomless.
3. "That spider is harmless," said the park ranger.

Grammar: The Future Continuous

Aim
· Develop the students' understanding of the simple and continuous tenses and introduce the future continuous (also called the future progressive).

Introduction
· Review the simple and continuous tenses covered so far. Draw a simple grid on the board with three boxes across the top and two boxes down, large enough to write a simple sentence in each box. Write in the tenses as you talk about them; start with the simple past, present, and future along the top row, then add the past and present continuous in the bottom row. Leave room for the future continuous in the bottom-right corner.
· Discuss with the students how each tense is formed.
· Remind them that the simple present describes an action that is repeated or usual (e.g. *She plays tennis twice a week*), while the present continuous describes something that has started and is still happening (e.g. *We are playing a game*).
· The simple past describes an action that started and finished within a specific time (e.g. *I walked to school today*), while the continuous past describes an action that had started and was still happening in the past (e.g. *I was walking to school when we met*).
· Say *I cook dinner* and ask the students which tense is being used. Write the sentence in the grid under *simple present*.
· Then ask them how the sentence would be written in the other tenses and write each one in the appropriate part of the grid (simple past: *I cooked dinner*; simple future: *I shall cook dinner*; past continuous: *I was cooking dinner*; present continuous: *I am cooking dinner*.)

Main Point
· Explain that the continuous tenses, like the simple tenses, can happen in the future as well as the past and present. On the board, write *future continuous* in the bottom-right corner of the grid.
· Like the past and present continuous, the future continuous is made by adding the present participle to the auxiliary verb *to be*.
· Ask the students what they think the future continuous of the sentence might be. Write *I shall be cooking dinner* to complete the grid.
· Underline *shall be* in red and remind the students that this is the future of *to be*.
· Conjugate *to cook* in the future continuous with the students (*I shall be cooking, you will be cooking, he/she/it will be cooking, we shall be cooking, you will be cooking, they will be cooking*), while doing the corresponding pronoun actions.

· Explain that the simple future describes an action which will start and finish within a specific time in the future, while the future continuous describes an action that will have started and will still be happening in the future.

Activity Page
· The students conjugate the sentence *I paint a picture* in the future continuous.
· Next they read the sentences and underline the verbs in red, remembering to underline all the parts of the verb, including the auxiliary ones.
· Finally, they read the sentences at the bottom of the page and join each one to the correct tense.

Extension Activity
· Write the following sentences on the board:
  1. *I was swimming in the pool.*
  2. *I shall be swimming in the pool.*
  3. *I swim in the pool.*
  4. *I shall swim in the pool.*
  5. *I swam in the pool.*
  6. *I am swimming in the pool.*
· The students read each sentence and decide which tense it is in.

Finishing the Lesson
· Read through the page with the students.

65

Spelling: The ‹-able› Suffix

Spelling Test
- The students turn to the backs of their books and find the column labeled *Spelling Test 17*.
- Call out the spelling words learned last week.

Review
- Review the soft ‹c›, soft ‹g›, ‹tch›, ‹dge›, ‹le›, and ‹qu› spellings, the ‹n› spelling of the /ng/ sound, and the ‹s›, ‹se›, and ‹ze› spellings of /z/. Blend and sound out the following words with the class, identifying the different spelling patterns: *pink, ce*real, *di*gital, *match, gadget, riddle, squeak, cosy, choose, sneeze*.

Spelling Point
- Review the suffix ‹-less›.
- Introduce the suffix ‹-able›, which is usually added to words (often verbs) to make adjectives.
- Words ending in ‹-able› describe something as being "capable or worthy of being (it)." So, *breakable* means *capable of being broken*, as in *That vase is breakable*.
- As ‹-able› starts with a vowel, the following rules apply when adding it to a root word:
  a. If the root word ends with a consonant that is not immediately preceded by a short vowel, simply add ‹-able›. So, *break* becomes *breakable*.
  b. If the root word ends in ‹e›, remove it before adding ‹-able› (e.g. *believable*). The exception is when the ‹e› is part of the soft ‹c› or soft ‹g› spelling (e.g. *noticeable, changeable*). Some words can be spelled either with or without the ‹e›, so both *lovable* and *loveable* are correct. However, in these cases it is better for the students to be consistent and drop the ‹e› in their writing.
  c. If the root word ends with a consonant that is immediately preceded by a short, stressed vowel sound, double the final consonant before adding ‹-able› (e.g. *controllable*).
  d. If the root word ends in a ‹y›, immediately preceded by a consonant (e.g. *vary*), replace the ‹y› with ‹i› before adding ‹-able› (e.g. *variable*).

Spelling List
- Read the spelling words with the students and identify the suffix ‹-able› in each one. Ask the class to highlight ‹-able›.
- Explain the meanings of any unfamiliar words. Point out that the ‹e› has been dropped in *usable, lovable, debatable,* and *desirable*, but not in *changeable* and *noticeable*.

avoidable
profitable
available
portable
adaptable
dependable
breakable
usable
lovable
irritable
enjoyable
debatable
changeable
disposable
desirable
miserable
variable
noticeable

Activity Page
- The students make new words by adding ‹-able› to the root word, applying the right spelling rules, and write them on the lines (*breakable, washable, valuable, sizable, enjoyable, reliable, suitable, comfortable, adorable, huggable, desirable, pitiable*).
- Next, the students use a dictionary to look up the words in the comfortable cushions. They read each definition and write the page numbers in the boxes.
- Then they identify the vowel sounds in the words and separate the words into syllables (*en/joy/a/ble, lov/a/ble, hug/ga/ble, re/li/a/ble, u/sa/ble*), and parse the sentences, underlining each part of speech in the correct color.
  The <u>dirty</u> <u>shirt</u> <u>is</u> <u>washable</u>.
  The <u>sofa</u> <u>was</u> <u>old</u> <u>but</u> <u>comfortable</u>.

Dictation
- Dictate the sentences below.
- Remind the students to use the correct punctuation in the second sentence. *May* is a proper noun and needs a capital letter. In the third sentence, *boy's* needs an apostrophe to show possession.
  1. They claimed the ship was unsinkable.
  2. "The kittens were all adorable," said May.
  3. It was improbable the boy's rocket would reach the moon.

Grammar: The ‹-less› and ‹-ful› Suffixes

Aim
- Refine the students' knowledge of suffixes and how they change the meaning of words.
- Introduce the suffix ‹-ful›.

Introduction
- Review suffixes. Remind the class that a suffix is usually one or more syllables added at the end of a word to change its meaning; they can be used to make plural nouns (e.g. *cups, boxes*), comparative and superlative adjectives (e.g. *bigger, biggest*), the simple past tense (e.g. *I wanted*), and the present participle (e.g. *walking*).
- Ask the students which new suffixes they have learned recently (‹-less› and ‹-able›) and review the spelling rules for adding them to root words (see pages 64 and 66).
- Write some ‹-able› and ‹-less› adjectives on the board and discuss their meanings with the class. Remind the students that adjectives ending in ‹-able› describe something as being "capable or worthy of being (it)," while adjectives ending in ‹-less› describe something as being "without (it)."

Main Point
- Write the word *pain* on the board and add the suffix ‹-less› to make *painless*. Ask the students what it means and how it could be used in a sentence.
- Now write the word *pain* again, but this time add the suffix ‹-ful› to make *painful*. Again, ask the students what it means and how they might use it in a sentence.
- Compare the two meanings and explain that when ‹-ful› and ‹-less› are added to words, they make adjectives with opposite meanings. The suffix ‹-less› means "without (it)" and the suffix ‹-ful› means "full of (it)."
- Ask the students for other words ending in ‹-less› and ‹-ful› which have opposite meanings.
- Remind the class that because both suffixes start with a consonant they are usually just added to the root word, except in a word like *pity*. If the root word ends in ‹y›, and a consonant immediately precedes it, "shy ‹i›" no longer needs "toughy ‹y›" to replace it, as it is no longer on the end of the word. (So, *pity* becomes *pitiful* or *pitiless*).

Activity Page
- The students read the root words in the fish bodies at the top of the page.
- They add the suffixes ‹-ful› and ‹-less› to make two adjectives with opposite meanings. They write these adjectives on the lines.

- Finally, the students write a sentence for each word to show its meaning.

Extension Activity
- Provide colored paper, pens, and scissors for the students to make their own "suffix fish." See the illustration on page 25 of this *Teacher's Book*.
- The students cut out three fish tail shapes and write a different suffix on each one: ‹-less›, ‹-able›, ‹-ful›.
- Next, they cut out as many fish body shapes (with heads) as they can and write a different root word in each one. Good examples of root words include the following: *worth, cloud, value, care, wonder, hope, use, end, bash, sink, vary, comfort, adjust, power, cheer, boast, motion, price, joy, pity, solve, beat, help, dispose, breath, desire, resist, avoid, depend, duty, time, pain, harm, face, name, beauty.*
- The students use the fish pieces to make new words, deciding which of the suffixes in the tails can be added to the words in the fish bodies to make new adjectives. They could also write the new words down and use some of them in sentences.

Finishing the Lesson
- Read through the page with the students and check their answers. Ask some of the students to read out their sentences.

Spelling: The ‹a› Spelling of the /ai/ Sound

Spelling Test
- The students turn to the backs of their books and find the column labeled *Spelling Test 18*.
- Call out the spelling words learned last week.

Review
- Use the "vowel hand" (see page 24) to review the five vowel letters and their short and long sounds.
- Write the following words on the board: s*tay*, *tail*, *male*, *crayon*, *escape*, *mainly*, *day*, *waiting*, *animate*, *praying*, *reindeer*, *eigh*t.
- Blend and sound out the words with the class, and identify the alternative spellings for the /ai/ sound.

Spelling Point
- Write *paper* on the board and ask which spelling is making the /ai/ sound. Slowly sound out the word, /p-ai-p-er/, and add the long vowel mark over the ‹a›.
- Explain that although the single vowel letter ‹a› usually makes the short /a/ sound, it can also make a long /ai/ sound. Sometimes this is because the short vowel sound in one syllable is made long by the "magic" from the vowel in the following syllable.
- In *paper*, point out how the magic from the ‹e› in /er/ has changed the short /a/ into a long /ai/ sound.
- However, this is not always the case. Write *pastry* on the board and underline the ‹str›. Remind the class that these consonants create a thick "wall" which prevents the "magic" from the ‹y› changing the ‹a›. This means that the ‹a› in *pastry* makes the /ai/ sound on its own, without any influence from other vowels.
- Now separate the words *paper* and *pastry* into syllables with a line (*pa/per*, *pa/stry*).
- Explain that syllables ending in a long vowel sound are called "open syllables," while syllables that end in a consonant (e.g. *rab/bit*) are called "closed syllables" and usually make a short vowel sound.

Spelling List
- Read the spelling words with the students and identify the ‹a› making an /ai/ sound in each word. The students highlight the ‹a› and put the long vowel mark over it.
- Explain the meanings of any unfamiliar words. Point out the ‹le› in *maple*, the ‹ue› in *plague*, the ‹ch› spelling of /k/ in *chaotic*, the soft ‹c› in *adjacent*, the ‹tion› in *conversation*, and the ‹s› in *newspaper*, which can say /z/.

crazy
taste
basic
baby
haste
maple
inhaler
pastry
acorn
stable
vacant
chamber
plague
chaotic
stranger
adjacent
newspaper
conversation

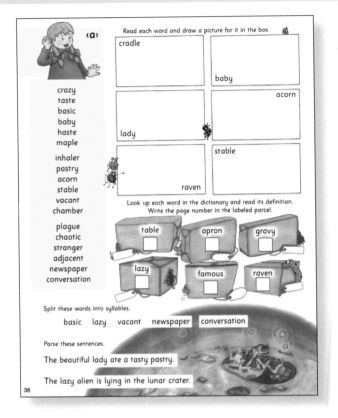

Activity Page
- The students read each word and illustrate it in the box. Next, the students use a dictionary to look up the words in the labeled boxes. They read each definition and write the page numbers in the boxes.
- Then they identify the vowel sounds in the words and separate the words into syllables (*ba/sic, la/zy, va/cant, news/pa/per, con/ver/sa/tion*).
- They parse the sentences, underlining each part of speech in the correct color. The second sentence is written in the present continuous, so both parts of the verb should be underlined in red.
The <u>beautiful</u> <u>lady</u> <u>ate</u> a <u>tasty</u> <u>pastry</u>.
The <u>lazy</u> <u>alien</u> <u>is lying</u> <u>in</u> the <u>lunar</u> <u>crater</u>.

Dictation
- Dictate the sentences below. Point out that the second sentence needs a question mark, and the third needs speech marks with the correct punctuation. *Dad* is a proper noun and needs a capital letter.

1. We had an apricot pastry for dessert.
2. Is the oak tree full of acorns?
3. "Put the paper on the table," said Dad.

Extension Activity
- The students make a list of words with the ‹a› spelling of the /ai/ sound in their Spelling Word Books.

Grammar: Contractions

Aim
- Refine the students' knowledge of contractions.
- Review how to use contractions in writing.

Introduction
- Remind the class that punctuation is important because it helps us make sense of the words we use.
- Ask the students what punctuation marks they know (periods, question marks, speech marks, exclamation marks, commas, and apostrophes).
- Review apostrophes and how they are positioned above the line in writing.
- Ask the students when they would use apostrophes. They could say that apostrophe ‹s› is used to show possession (e.g. *Danny's cat*), or that an apostrophe can be used to show that one or more letters is missing.
- Remind the students that this happens sometimes when we shorten a pair of words and join them together (e.g. *does not* becomes *doesn't*), and when we make a single word shorter (e.g. *cannot* becomes *can't*). Remind the class that when we do this, it is called a contraction.
- Contractions are mostly used in speech; they should not be used in writing except when writing speech or a friendly note.

Main Point
- Contractions are often used when a spoken sentence is describing a future action.
- Write *You will be walking the dog* on the board, and ask the students which words are making the verb (*will be walking*) and what tense this is (the future continuous).
- Conjugate the sentence with the class (*I shall be walking the dog, you will be walking the dog, he/she/it will be walking the dog,* and so on).
- Explain that, while this is how the students would write the sentence, it is probably not what they would say to someone. It is more likely that they would shorten it to *You'll be walking the dog,* by joining together the words *you* and *will* to make *you'll*.
- Ask the students which letters have been left out. Erase ‹wi› and put an apostrophe in its place.
- Go through the other contractions with the class (*I shall/I'll, he will/he'll, she will/she'll, it will/it'll, we shall/we'll, you will/you'll, they will/they'll*).
- Point out that in *I'll* and *we'll* the letters that have been removed are the ‹sha› from *shall* rather than the ‹wi› from *will*.

Activity Page
- The students write each pair of words as a contraction

by joining them together and replacing the ‹wi› or ‹sha› with an apostrophe.
- Next, they rewrite the sentences, writing each contraction as two words and with no letters missing. Then the students rewrite the last two sentences using contractions.
- Finally, they write inside the outlined words *I'll, you'll, she'll, we'll,* and *they'll*.

Extension Activity
- Write the following word pairs and corresponding contractions onto small pieces of card: *is not/isn't, cannot/can't, did not/didn't, does not/doesn't, have not/haven't, I shall/I'll, he will/he'll, she will/she'll, it will/it'll, we shall/we'll, you will/you'll, they will/they'll*. It might be helpful to make more than one set of cards.
- The students work in pairs, taking it in turns to choose a card and read it out. If they read out a word pair, their partner has to say the corresponding contraction and spell it. If it is a contraction, the partner has to say it in full as two words (or as the whole word in the case of *can't/cannot*).
- Alternatively, the students could play "pairs," or write sentences using the words and contractions.

Finishing the Lesson
- Read through the page with the students.

Spelling: The ‹e› Spelling of the /ee/ Sound

Spelling Test
- The students turn to the backs of their books and find the column labeled *Spelling Test 19*.
- In any order, call out the spelling words learned last week. The students write the words on the lines.

Review
- Use the "vowel hand" (see page 24) to review the five vowel letters and their short and long sounds.
- Write the following words on the board: *gene, reach, sleep, teacher, theme, coffee, beam, agreement, compete, seagull, sunny, donkey, thief*.
- Blend and sound out the words with the class, and identify the alternative spellings for the /ee/ sound.

Spelling Point
- Write *prefix* on the board and add the long vowel mark over the ‹e›. Explain that although the single vowel letter ‹e› usually makes the short /e/ sound, it can also make a long /ee/ sound.
- Ask the students what is making the ‹e› in *prefix* say /ee/. (It is the "magic" from the ‹i› in the second syllable.)
- However, this is not always the case. Write *secret* on the board and underline the ‹cr›. Remind the class that these consonants create a thick "wall" which prevents the "magic" from the second ‹e› changing the first ‹e›. The ‹e› in *secret* makes the /ee/ sound on its own, without any influence from other vowels.
- Now separate the word *prefix* into syllables with a line (*pre/fix*). The second syllable is a "closed syllable" as it ends in a consonant and has a short /i/, while the first syllable is an "open syllable" as it ends in a long /ee/. This is why the ‹e› in the monosyllabic tricky words *he, she, me, we, be*, and *the* also make the long /ee/ sound.

Spelling List
- Read the spelling words with the students and identify the ‹e› making an /ee/ sound in each word. The students highlight the ‹e› and put the long vowel mark over it.
- Explain the meanings of any unfamiliar words.
- Emphasize the ‹al› in *legal, regal,* and *medieval*. Point out the soft ‹c› in *recent*, the ‹qu› in *frequent*, and the ‹ch› spelling of /k/ in *chameleon*. It may help the students to remember the ‹e› spelling of /ee/ if they put the words together in a silly sentence.

evil
email
secret
legal
fever
regal
female
prefect
recent
media
create
medium
frequent
adhesive
medieval
chameleon
immediate
prehistoric

Activity Page
- The students put the words from the spelling list into alphabetical order (*adhesive, chameleon, create, email, evil, female, fever, frequent, immediate, legal, media, medieval, medium, prefect, prehistoric, recent, regal, secret*).
- Next, the students use a dictionary to look up the words in the shields. They read each definition and write the page numbers in the boxes.
- Then they identify the vowel sounds in the words and separate the words into syllables (*re/flex, e/mail, fe/male, ge/ni/us, fre/quent*).
- They parse the sentences, underlining each part of speech in the correct color. The first sentence is written in the future continuous, so all parts of the verb should be underlined in red.
  She will be visiting her grandparents.
  An emu is a large Australian bird.

Dictation
- Dictate the sentences below. Remind them to use speech marks with the correct punctuation in the first sentence.

1. "I think I have a fever," she said.
2. They kept his birthday present a secret.
3. He will be sending an email to his friend.

Grammar: Comparatives and Superlatives

Aim
• Reinforce the students' knowledge of adjectives. Review how to make positive adjectives into comparative and superlative adjectives.

Introduction
• Review adjectives and the action for them (touch the side of your temple with your fist).
• Adjectives are words that describe nouns (or pronouns) and the color for them is blue.
• Write some nouns on the board (e.g. *cat, car, book, shirt, dragon, castle, tent*) and ask for some adjectives to describe them. The nouns chosen could be from a topic the students are studying.

Main Point
• Remind the students that they know two special sorts of adjective called comparatives and superlatives, which describe a noun by comparing it with one or more other items.
• Draw a picture of an elephant, for example, on the board. Write *This is a big elephant* underneath, and underline the adjective *big* in blue.
• Now draw a slightly bigger elephant and ask the students to describe it. Hopefully, they will say it is bigger. Write *This elephant is bigger,* and underline the comparative adjective *bigger* in blue.
• Now draw an even bigger elephant. Write *This is the biggest elephant,* and underline the superlative adjective *biggest* in blue. Point out that the definite article, *the,* is needed for the superlative.
• Remind the class that a comparative adjective is made by adding the suffix ‹-er› to the root word, and means "more [adjective]." A superlative adjective is made by adding the suffix ‹-est› to the root word, and means "most [adjective]." As both suffixes start with a vowel, the students must remember to use the same spelling rules as for adding ‹-ed› (see page 25). For the word *big,* for example, they must use the "doubling" rule, as the word ends in a consonant preceded by a short, stressed vowel sound, so the ‹g› is doubled to make *bigger.*
• With the students, practice making comparatives and superlatives from other adjectives. (You could use the adjectives discussed at the beginning of the lesson, or ask for more suggestions).
• Ask the students which spelling they would use in each case. For example, with a word like *brave* they must remember to remove the ‹e› before adding ‹-er› and ‹-est› (*brave, braver, bravest*); with a word like *gray,* where the word ends in a vowel followed by ‹y›, they should simply add the suffix (*gray, grayer, grayest*); with a word like *happy,* they must remember that

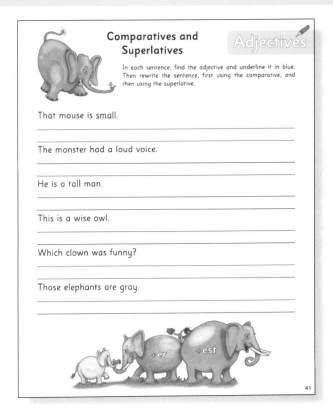

"shy ‹i›" replaces "toughy ‹y›," as it is no longer on the end of the word (*happy, happier, happiest*).
• End this activity with a longer adjective (e.g. *enormous*). Ask the students how they would make the comparative and superlative for this word. Explain that short adjectives of one or two syllables take the ‹-er› and ‹-est› suffixes, while longer ones often use the words *more* and *most.* So, we say *bigger* and *biggest,* but *more enormous* and *most enormous.*

Activity Page
• The students read the sentences and identify the adjective in each one. Next the students look at each adjective and write the sentence again, first using the comparative adjective and then the superlative (e.g. *That mouse is small. That mouse is smaller. That mouse is the smallest*). Remind the students to use the appropriate spelling rules when adding the suffixes.

Extension Activity
• Provide a sheet of paper for each student.
• The students choose an adjective and write three sentences of their own, using the adjective, the comparative, and then the superlative. They draw pictures to illustrate their three sentences.

Finishing the Lesson
• Read through the page with the students.

Spelling: The ‹i› Spelling of the /ie/ Sound

Spelling Test
- The students turn to the backs of their books and find the column labeled *Spelling Test 20*.
- Call out the spelling words learned last week.

Review
- Use the "vowel hand" (see page 24) to review the five vowel letters and their short and long sounds.
- Write the following words on the board: *life, high, sty, tied, reply, right, fire, fly, flies, asylum.*
- Blend and sound out the words with the class, and identify the alternative spellings for the /ie/ sound.

Spelling Point
- Remind the students that although a single vowel letter usually makes a short sound, it can also make a long sound. Sometimes this is because the short vowel sound in one syllable is changed by the "magic" from the vowel in the next syllable (e.g. *final*). However, sometimes the short vowel letter makes the long vowel sound on its own, without any influence from other vowels (e.g. *child*).
- Write *li/on* on the board and point out that the first syllable ends in a vowel, so ‹i› makes the long /ie/ sound. The second syllable ends in ‹n›, so ‹o› says its short vowel sound (although it is really pronounced as a schwa). Ask the students what kind of syllables these are (an "open syllable" and a "closed syllable").
- Now write *di/et* on the board. Explain that the students need to take care when two vowels come together in a word with more than one syllable. They will be familiar with the idea that "when two vowels go walking, the first does the talking," as in /ai/, /ee/, /ie/, /oa/, and /ue/. However, in some words the second vowel also has its own sound. In *diet*, the ‹ie› does not represent one sound, /ie/, but two vowel sounds, /ie/ and /e/ (more commonly a schwa), which makes it a two-syllable word.

Spelling List
- Read the spelling words with the students and identify the ‹i› making an /ie/ sound in each word. The students highlight the ‹i› and put the long vowel mark over it. Explain the meanings of any unfamiliar words.
- Point out the ‹y› in *icy*, the ‹ph› in *phial* and *microphone*, the ‹qu› in *quiet*, the soft ‹g› in *gigantic*, and the ‹al› in *diagonal*.

icy
icon
diet
child
idea
wild
behind
spider
pirate
diary
Viking
horizon
phial
quiet
gigantic
diagonal
microphone
hibernate

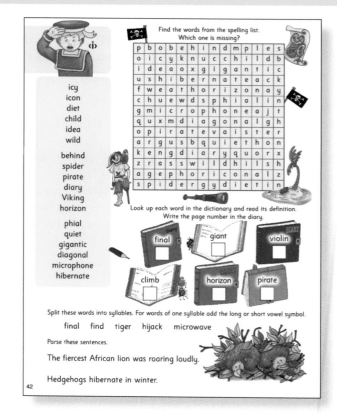

icy
icon
diet
child
idea
wild

behind
spider
pirate
diary
Viking
horizon

phial
quiet
gigantic
diagonal
microphone
hibernate

Find the words from the spelling list. Which one is missing?

Look up each word in the dictionary and read its definition. Write the page number in the diary.

final · giant · violin · climb · horizon · pirate

Split these words into syllables. For words of one syllable add the long or short vowel symbol.

final · find · tiger · hijack · microwave

Parse these sentences.

The fiercest African lion was roaring loudly.

Hedgehogs hibernate in winter.

42

- Explain that *Viking* is both a proper noun and a proper adjective.

Activity Page
- The students find the words from the spelling list in the word search and work out which word is missing (*Viking*). Next, they use a dictionary to look up the words in the diaries. They read each definition and write the page numbers in the boxes. Then they identify the vowel sounds in the words and separate the words into syllables (*fi/nal, ti/ger, hi/jack, mi/cro/wave*). They put the long vowel mark over the ‹i› in *find*. Finally, the students parse the sentences, underlining each part of speech in the correct color. The first sentence is written in the past continuous, so both parts of the verb should be underlined in red. The <u>fiercest</u> <u>African</u> <u>lion</u> <u>was roaring</u> <u>loudly</u>. <u>Hedgehogs</u> <u>hibernate</u> <u>in</u> <u>winter</u>.

Dictation
- Dictate the sentences below. Remind the class to use speech marks with the correct punctuation in the first sentence. *Tibetan*, in the second sentence, is a proper adjective and needs a capital letter.

1. "I had a wild time," yelled the child.
2. They went climbing in the Tibetan mountains.
3. The giant was playing a violin.

Grammar: *Adverbs* *(Made by Adding ‹-ly› to Adjectives)*

Aim
• Develop the students' awareness that many adjectives can be made into adverbs by adding the suffix ‹-ly›.

Introduction
• Review nouns and adjectives, including comparatives and superlatives, as well as verbs and adverbs (see pages 6 to 13 of this *Teacher's Book*).
• Remind the students that just as adjectives describe nouns (or pronouns), so adverbs are words that describe verbs; they tell us how, when, or where an action is performed. Check that the students remember the color for adverbs (orange) and its action (the students bang one fist on top of the other).
• Ask the class to suggest some verbs and write them on the board. Look at the verbs in turn and ask the students to think of a different adverb each time to describe them.

Main Point
• Remind the students that when a suffix (or prefix) is added to a word, it changes its meaning.
• Point out that the addition of a suffix (or prefix) can also change the kind of word it is. Explain that the suffix ‹-ly› can be added to many adjectives to make them into adverbs.
• Write an adjective (e.g. *slow*) on the board and ask the students to suggest a sentence using the word (e.g. *This is a slow train*).
• Now add ‹-ly› to *slow* to make *slowly*. Ask a student to suggest a sentence using the new word (e.g. *The train moves slowly*).
• Compare how the two words are used in the sentences (in this example, *slow* describes the train itself, but *slowly* describes how the train is moving).
• Think of some other adjectives that can be made into adverbs by adding ‹-ly›, and write them on the board (e.g. *odd, patient, regular, special, fluent, sweet, nervous, perfect, slow, bad, calm, general, thick, polite, bright, graceful, soft, beautiful, stubborn, foolish, sudden, continuous, unexpected*).
• Add ‹-ly› to each one and ask the students to think of a sentence using each adverb.
• As ‹-ly› begins with a consonant, it is usually just added to the root word, although there are a few exceptions:
- If a word ends in a consonant followed by a ‹y›, "shy ‹i›" replaces "toughy ‹y›" before the ‹-ly› is added (e.g. *happy/happily, heavy/heavily, easy/easily, messy/messily*).
- If a word ends in ‹le›, the ‹le› is removed before adding ‹-ly› (e.g. *simple/simply, idle/idly, gentle/gently, reasonable/reasonably*).

- If a word ends in ‹ic›, the suffix ‹-ally› is added instead of ‹-ly› (e.g. *frantic/frantically, dramatic/dramatically, specific/specifically*).
• It is important that the students understand that not all words ending in ‹-ly› are adverbs; some adjectives end in ‹-ly› as well (e.g. *friendly, lively, elderly, lonely, silly, lovely*). There are also many adverbs that do not end in ‹-ly› (e.g. *high, late, soon, always, well*).

Activity Page
• The students make each adjective into an adverb by adding ‹-ly›. They write the new adverbs in the table.
• Next they read each sentence, identify the adjective, and complete each second sentence by writing the corresponding adverb on the line.
• Lastly, the students choose three adverbs from the flowers and use each one in a sentence.

Extension Activity
• Write some more adjectives on the board and ask the students to make them into adverbs by adding ‹-ly›. Remind them to use the appropriate spelling rules.
• The students could also write a few sentences using some of the adverbs.

Finishing the Lesson
• Read through the page with the students.

73

Spelling: The ‹o› Spelling of the /oa/ Sound

Spelling Test
- The students turn to the backs of their books and find the column labeled *Spelling Test 21*.
- Call out the spelling words learned last week.

Review
- Use the "vowel hand" (see page 24) to review the five vowel letters and their short and long sounds.
- Write the following words on the board: *float, elbow, owner, alone, follow, moan, tadpole, shadow, rainbow, millstone*.
- Blend and sound out the words with the class, and identify the alternative spellings for the /oa/ sound.

Spelling Point
- Remind the students that although a single vowel letter usually makes a short sound, it can also make a long sound. Sometimes this is because the short vowel sound in one syllable is changed by the "magic" from the vowel in the next syllable (e.g. *total*). However, sometimes the short vowel letter makes the long vowel sound on its own, without any influence from other vowels (e.g. *only*).
- Write *cro/cus* on the board and point out that the first syllable ends in a vowel, so the ‹o› makes a long /oa/ sound. The second syllable ends in ‹s›, so the ‹u› makes its short vowel sound. Ask the students what kind of syllables these are (an "open syllable" and a "closed syllable," respectively).
- Now write *po/em* on the board. Remind the class that although it is often true that "when two vowels go walking, the first does the talking," in some words the second vowel also has its own sound. Here, the ‹oe› has two vowel sounds, /oa/ and /e/ (more commonly a schwa), which makes *poem* a two-syllable word.

Spelling List
- Read the spelling words with the students and identify the /oa/ sound in each word. The students highlight the ‹o› and put the long vowel mark over it. Explain the meanings of any unfamiliar words. Emphasize the ‹a› in *oval* and *total*. Point out the ‹y› saying /ee/ in *only*, *anchovy*, and *vocabulary*, the ‹re› in *ogre*, and the ‹i› at the end of *macaroni*. (This is unusual in English but *macaroni* is derived from Italian). Explain that *Roman* is both a proper noun and a proper adjective and needs a capital letter.

open
oval
only
poem
total
clover
mosaic
cocoa
mobile
Roman
pronoun
moment
ogre
anchovy
overboard
vocabulary
macaroni
steamroller

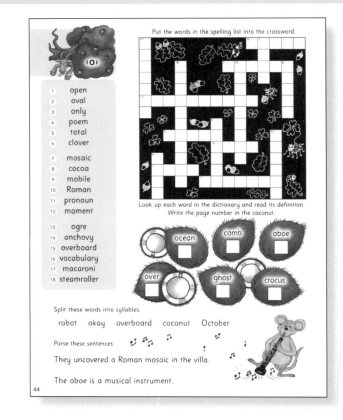

Put the words in the spelling list into the crossword.

1 open
2 oval
3 only
4 poem
5 total
6 clover
7 mosaic
8 cocoa
9 mobile
10 Roman
11 pronoun
12 moment
13 ogre
14 anchovy
15 overboard
16 vocabulary
17 macaroni
18 steamroller

Look up each word in the dictionary and read its definition. Write the page number in the coconut.

ocean   comb   oboe
over   ghost   crocus

Split these words into syllables.
robot   okay   overboard   coconut   October

Parse these sentences.
They uncovered a Roman mosaic in the villa.
The oboe is a musical instrument.

44

Activity Page
- The students fill in the crossword using the words from the spelling list. (The numbers in the crossword indicate the correct word from the spelling list.)
- Next, the students use a dictionary to look up the words in the coconuts. They read each definition and write the page numbers in the boxes. The students could also write down the meanings for some of the words.
- Then they identify the vowel sounds in the words and separate the words into syllables (*ro/bot, o/kay, o/ver/board, co/co/nut, Oc/to/ber*).
- Finally, the students parse the sentences, underlining each part of speech in the correct color.
  They uncovered a Roman mosaic in the villa.
  The oboe is a musical instrument.

Dictation
- Provide a sheet of paper for each student and dictate the following sentences:

  1. They both went to the local school.
  2. He folded the paper over.
  3. She was hoping to find some clover.

Extension Activity
- The students make a list of words with the ‹o› spelling of the /oa/ sound in their Spelling Word Books.

Grammar: Nouns Acting as Adjectives

Aim
• Develop the students' awareness that nouns can sometimes act as adjectives in a sentence.

Introduction
• Review compound words. Remind the students that compound words are made up of two (or more) shorter words joined together.
• Ask the students for some examples and write them on the board (e.g. *blackbird, starfish, football, toadstool, toothbrush, seahorse, butterfly, lighthouse*).
• Identify the short words making each compound word and discuss how putting them together changes the meaning of the word.
• Explain that in a compound word the first word is usually describing (or modifying) the second. It is often describing its quality (what it is like) or its purpose (what it is for); a *blackbird* is a type of bird that is black, and a *toothbrush* is a type of brush for cleaning teeth.
• It is not always possible to understand a compound word simply by knowing the words in it; seahorses are not really horses that live in the sea and starfish are not really fish, although it is easy to see how they got their names. In the case of other compound words, like *toadstool* and *butterfly*, the origin of the word is much less clear.

Main Point
• Tell the students that compound words are not always written as one word. Sometimes they have a small line separating the smaller words, called a hyphen (e.g. *mother-in-law*), and sometimes they are written as separate words (e.g. *bus stop*). Sometimes, the same word can be written in all of these ways (e.g. *lifestyle, life-style, life style*). So, the best way to be sure is to look in a dictionary.
• Write the following sentence on the board: *Granny made an apple pie.* Parse the words *Granny* (noun, black) and *made* (verb, red) with the students.
• Now look at the last two words. Explain that *apple pie* is a compound word made from the words *apple* and *pie*. Although the word *apple* is a noun, here it is describing what kind of pie Granny made, so it is doing the job of an adjective.
• Point out that other nouns could describe the pie without changing the basic meaning of the sentence (i.e. that Granny made a pie). Ask the students for some suggestions (e.g. *peach, cherry, blackberry, fish, steak, chicken, and mushroom*).
• Finish parsing the sentence with the students. Underline the word *apple* in blue because it is doing the job of an adjective, and the noun *pie* in black.

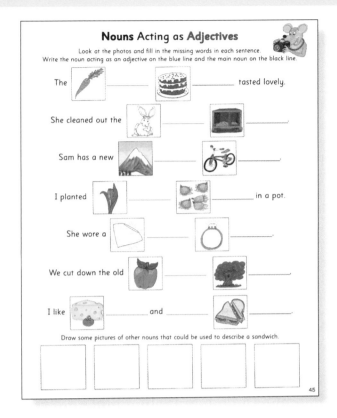

Activity Page
• The students complete each sentence by writing the missing words (indicated by the pictures) on the lines to make the compound word.
• The students then think of some nouns that could be used to describe a sandwich (e.g. *egg, cucumber, salmon, chicken*). They illustrate these in the boxes.

Extension Activity
• Provide some paper for the students.
• Write the following nouns on the board: *pie, ball, soup, box, race, juice.*
• The students choose one of the nouns from the board and write it in the middle of their sheet of paper, underlining it in black.
• Then they think of some more nouns that could act as adjectives for this noun and write them around the main noun, underlining them in blue. They might suggest: *apple, cherry, fish,* or *chicken* for pie; *tennis, golf, beach,* or *crystal* for ball; *onion, vegetable, mushroom,* or *potato* for soup; *music, jewelry, window,* or *toy* for box; *horse, boat, sack,* or *obstacle* for race; *fruit, orange, lemon,* or *tomato* for juice.
• Lastly, they illustrate each noun underneath.

Finishing the Lesson
• Read through the page with the students and check their answers.

Spelling: The ‹-o› Spelling of the /oa/ Sound

Spelling Test
- The students turn to the backs of their books and find the column labeled *Spelling Test 22*.
- Call out the spelling words learned last week.

Review
- Use the "vowel hand" (see page 24) to review the five vowel letters and their short and long sounds.
- Blend and sound out the following words with the class, identifying the alternative spelling for the /oa/ sound in each one: *froze, foal, stone, mobile, snow, yellow, comb, globe, toadstool, robot.*

Spelling Point
- Write *volcano* on the board and remind the students that although the single vowel letter ‹o› usually makes its short sound /o/, it can also make the long sound /oa/ (see page 74).
- Separate *volcano* into syllables (*vol/ca/no*). Point out that the first syllable ends in a consonant so it is a "closed syllable." The other two syllables end in a long vowel sound, so they are "open syllables."
- Discuss how the ‹a› in *volcano* is changed by the ‹o› that comes after it, whereas the final ‹o› makes its long sound on its own. Look at some more words ending in ‹o› with the class (e.g. *bingo, cargo, disco, indigo, motto, potato, stereo, studio*) and explain that as each ‹o› comes at the end of the last syllable, it makes the long /oa/ sound.
- Tell the students that if a noun ends in ‹o›, the plural is usually made by adding ‹-s› or ‹-es›. Most words can use either suffix but there are exceptions: *torpedo, tomato,* and *potato*, for example, only use the ‹-es› plural. For this reason, it is better for the students to be consistent and always add ‹-es›. The only exception is when a word is foreign or an abbreviation (e.g. *piano, photo, disco, kilo, hippo*) or when there is a vowel immediately before the final ‹o› (e.g. *studio, radio, video*). These words always use the suffix ‹-s› for the plural.

Spelling List
- Read the spelling words with the students and identify the ‹o› making the /oa/ sound at the end of each word. The students highlight the ‹o› and put the long vowel mark over it. Explain the meanings of any unfamiliar words.
- Point out the ‹i› saying /ee/ in *pianos*,

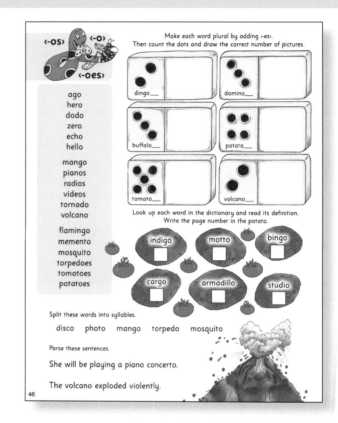

ago
hero
dodo
zero
echo
hello
mango
pianos
radios
videos
tornado
volcano
flamingo
memento
mosquito
torpedoes
tomatoes
potatoes

radios, and *mosquito*, and the ‹n› saying /ng/ in *flamingo*. Identify the different plural spellings.

Activity Page
- The students make each word plural by adding ‹-es› and draw the correct number of pictures.
- Next, the students use a dictionary to look up the words in the potatoes. They read each definition and write the page numbers in the boxes.
- Then they identify the vowel sounds in the words and separate the words into syllables (*dis/co, pho/to, man/go, tor/pe/do, mos/qui/to*).
- Finally, the students parse the sentences, underlining each part of speech in the correct color. The first sentence is written in the future continuous, so all parts of the verb should be underlined in red. *Piano* is a noun acting as an adjective and should be underlined in blue. She will be playing a piano concerto. The volcano exploded violently.

Dictation
- Dictate the sentences below. Remind the class to use speech marks with the correct punctuation in the first sentence.

1. "Hello," said the little boy.
2. The cracker had a hat and a motto in it.
3. Twelve minus zero equals twelve.

Grammar: *Adjectives* (Made by Adding ‹-y› to Nouns)

Aim
- Develop the students' awareness that many nouns can be made into adjectives by adding the suffix ‹-y›.

Introduction
- Review nouns and adjectives. Remind the students that adjectives are words that describe nouns (or pronouns), and check that they know the colors and actions for both (see pages 6 and 11 of this *Teacher's Book*).
- Ask the class to suggest some nouns and write them on the board. Look at each noun in turn and ask the students to think of an adjective to describe it. Write the adjective next to the noun and underline it in blue.
- Review how adjectives can be made into adverbs by adding ‹-ly›.
- Write the following sentence on the board, *It was a soft cushion.* Ask what sort of word *soft* is (it is an adjective describing the noun *cushion*).
- Now ask whether anyone can remember how to make an adverb from the adjective *soft*. Write *soft* on the board and add ‹-ly› to make the adverb *softly*.
- Ask the class for a sentence using this word (e.g. *She hummed softly*).

Main Point
- Explain that just as some adjectives can be made into adverbs by adding a suffix, so some nouns can be made into adjectives by adding the suffix ‹-y›.
- Write the word *sand* on the board and put it into a sentence: for example, *The sand on the beach was very hot.*
- Now write *I made a fantastic sandcastle* and ask what job the noun *sand* is doing in this compound word (it is describing the word *castle* so it is doing the job of an adjective).
- Add ‹-y› to the word *sand* on the board to make the adjective *sandy*. Ask the students to use it in a sentence, such as *I have sandy feet* or *My feet got sandy on the beach.*
- Parse the sentence with the students and identify *sandy* as an adjective, underlining it in blue.
- Choose some other nouns and make them into adjectives (e.g. *snowy, windy, frosty, silvery, sugary, roomy, flowery, watery, hilly, grassy, woody, milky, stormy, summery, dirty, hairy, weedy, leafy, creamy, sleepy*).
- Remind the students that there are usually some spelling rules for adding a suffix. For example, with words like *rose* and *noise*, they must remember to remove the ‹e› before adding ‹-y› to make *rosy* and *noisy*.

- With words like *sun, spot,* and *fog* the students must use the "doubling" rule. As each of these words ends in a consonant after a short, stressed vowel sound, the consonant is doubled to make *sunny, spotty,* and *foggy*.

Activity Page
- The students make each noun into an adjective by adding ‹-y›. They write the adjectives in the table.
- Next they read each sentence, identify the noun, and complete each second sentence by writing the corresponding adjective on the line.
- Lastly, the students choose three adjectives from the snakes and use each one in a sentence.

Extension Activity
- Write some more nouns on the board and ask the students to make them into adjectives by adding ‹-y›. Remind them to use the appropriate spelling rules.
- The students could also write a few sentences using some of the adjectives.

Finishing the Lesson
- Read through the page with the students, asking some of them to read out their sentences.

Spelling: The ‹u› Spelling of the /ue/ Sound

Spelling Test
- The students turn to the backs of their books and find the column labeled *Spelling Test 23*.
- In any order, call out the spelling words learned last week. The students write the words on the lines.

Review
- Use the "vowel hand" (see page 24) to review the five vowel letters and their short and long sounds.
- Blend and sound out the following words with the class, identifying the spelling of the /ue/ and long /oo/ sounds in each one: *cue, fewer, June, amuse, rescue, useless, newt, tuneless, blue, stew.*

Spelling Point
- Remind the students that although a single vowel letter usually makes a short sound, it can also make a long sound. Sometimes this is because the short vowel sound in one syllable is changed by the "magic" from the vowel in the next syllable (e.g. *unit*). However, sometimes the short vowel letter makes the long vowel sound on its own, without any influence from other vowels (e.g. *menu*).
- Write *cu/cum/ber* on the board and point out that the first syllable is an "open syllable" ending in a long /ue/ sound, but the second syllable is a "closed syllable" with a short /u/ sound.
- Now write *du/et* on the board. Remind the class that although it is often true that "when two vowels go walking, the first does the talking," in some words the second vowel also has its own sound. Here the ‹ue› has two vowel sounds, /ue/ and /e/, which makes *duet* a two-syllable word.

Spelling List
- Read the spelling words with the students and identify the ‹u› making either a /ue/ or long /oo/ sound in each word. The students highlight the ‹u› and put the long vowel mark over it. Explain the meanings of any unfamiliar words. Point out the ‹e› in *emu*, the ‹s› saying /z/ in *music*, the ‹s› saying /zh/ in *usual*, the soft ‹c›, ‹y›, and ‹le› in *unicycle* and the ‹tion› in *solution*. Emphasize the ‹al› in *usual*.
- It may help the students to remember the ‹u› spelling of /ue/ if they put the words together in a silly sentence. It is a good idea to blend and sound out the spelling words quickly every day with the students.

Spelling List
unit
tuna
duet
menu
tulip
emu
human
music
usual
computer
unicorn
unicycle
peculiar
cucumber
unique
universe
communicate
solution

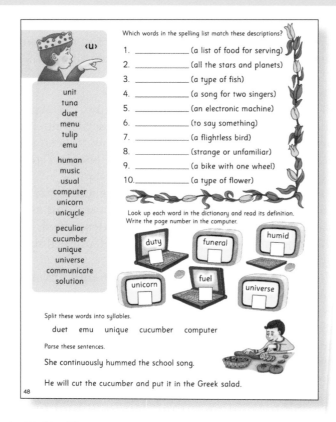

Activity Page
- The students read the phrases and decide which words from the spelling list they describe.
- Next, they use a dictionary to look up the words in the computers. They read each definition and write the page numbers in the boxes.
- Then they identify the vowel sounds in the words and separate the words into syllables (*du/et, e/mu, u/nique, cu/cum/ber, com/pu/ter*).
- Finally, the students parse the sentences, underlining each part of speech in the correct color. Point out that *school* is a noun acting as an adjective and should be underlined in blue. The second sentence is written in the simple future, so both parts of the verb should be underlined in red.

  She continuously hummed the school song.
  He will cut the cucumber and put it in the Greek salad.

Dictation
- Dictate the sentences below. Remind the class to use speech marks with the correct punctuation in the first sentence. *Granny* is a proper noun and needs a capital letter.

1. "I sent an email on my computer," Granny said proudly.
2. We saw an unusual monument.
3. The policeman was on duty all night.

Grammar: *Irregular Plurals*

Aim
- Develop the students' knowledge of plural words by reviewing how to make regular plurals, and introducing some common irregular plurals.

Introduction
- Review nouns. Remind the students that nouns can be singular (when there is only one of something) or plural (when there are more than one of something).
- The way a plural is usually made is by adding a suffix to the noun. Ask the students which suffixes they know that can make a plural, and review any they are unsure of.
  - The simplest way to make a plural is by adding ‹-s› to the end of a noun (e.g. *dog/dogs, house/houses, car/cars*).
  - If a noun ends in ‹ch›, ‹sh›, ‹s›, ‹z›, or ‹x›, then ‹-es› is added (e.g. *watch/watches, bush/bushes, glass/glasses, box/boxes*).
  - If a noun ends in ‹o›, then ‹-es› is usually added (e.g. *tomato/tomatoes, potato/potatoes, tornado/tornadoes*), except when the word is foreign, abbreviated, or has a vowel before the ‹o›, when ‹-s› is added (e.g. *disco/discos, kilo/kilos, studio/studios*).
  - If a noun ends in ‹y›, there are two options. If there is a vowel before the ‹y›, simply add ‹-s› (e.g. *boy/boys, day/days, key/keys*), but if there is a consonant before ‹y›, replace ‹y› with "shy ‹i›" before adding ‹-es› (e.g. *cherry/cherries, fly/flies, party/parties*).

Main Point
- The plurals introduced so far are all examples of "regular" plurals. They are regular because the students know how to make the plurals by following some simple rules. Explain that not all plurals are made in this way. Some plurals are irregular or "tricky" and have to be learned.
- Write the word *sheep* on the board and ask the students to think of its plural. If they find this difficult, prompt them, saying *One sheep and a flock of…* (*sheep*).
- Tell the students that some words are the same whether they are singular or plural. Ask them if they can think of any other nouns like this (e.g. *deer, fish, moose, salmon*). Point out that these words are often the names of animals. (*Fish* can also take the plural *fishes*, as in *all the little fishes*. Although it is more usual to say *I bought some fish; We caught three fish*.)
- Now write *foot, mouse,* and *man* on the board and ask the students for their plurals (*feet, mice, men*).
- Explain that many irregular plurals change some of the letters, usually those spelling the vowel sound.

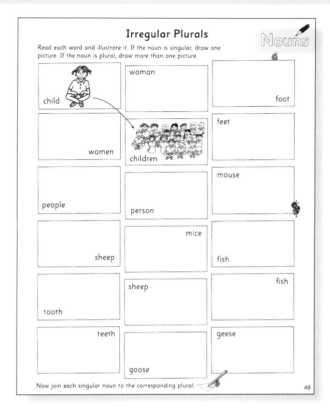

- Add *children* and *people* to the board, ask what the singular nouns for these are (*child, person*). Point out that some nouns have very irregular plurals.
- With the students, look at the *Student Book* page and discuss the other words with irregular plurals.

Activity Page
- The students read the word in each box, decide whether it is singular or plural, and draw one, or more than one, of the items.
- Then they join the singular nouns to their corresponding plurals.

Extension Activity
- Write the following plural nouns on the board: *deer, moose, radios, hippos, photos, tomatoes, tornadoes, daisies, babies, brushes, cherries, arches, buses, foxes, dresses, brushes, keys, donkeys, pies, bikes, acorns*.
- The students copy them out and write the corresponding singular nouns next to the plurals.
- Alternatively, they could write some sentences using some of the singular and plural nouns.

Finishing the Lesson
- Go around the class, checking that the students have correctly matched up the irregular plurals.
- If the students have written sentences, ask some of them to read them out.

Spelling: ‹aw› and ‹au› Making the /o/ Sound

Spelling Test
- The students turn to the backs of their books and find the column labeled *Spelling Test 24*.
- Call out the spelling words learned last week.

Review
- Write the following words on the board and blend and sound them out with the class: *cheese, easy, apple, anger, baby, evil, icy, ogre, ago, units*.
- Identify the spelling patterns: ‹se› and ‹s› saying /z/, ‹le› saying /ool/, ‹n› saying /ng/, and the vowel letters ‹a›, ‹e›, ‹i›, ‹o›, ‹u› saying their long sounds (as well as the soft ‹c› in *icy*).

Spelling Point
- Review the main ways of writing the /o/ sound and write them on the board: ‹o›, ‹aw›, ‹au›, ‹al›.
- Ask the students to suggest words for each alternative spelling. As each word is called out, ask the students which spelling it takes and add it to the appropriate column. Possible words include: ‹aw› *saw, claw, dawn, prawn, strawberry*; ‹au› *fault, autumn, haunt, August, astronaut, haul, launch, vault*; ‹al› *walk, talk, stalk, wall, call, halt, salt*. Point out that in some ‹al› words, the letter ‹l› is also pronounced (e.g. *halt, salt*).

Spelling List
- Read the spelling words with the students and identify the letters making the /o/ sound in each one. Ask the class to highlight the letters making the /o/ sound. Explain the meanings of any unfamiliar words.
- Point out the ‹k› spelling in *hawk* and *awkward*, the soft ‹c› in *sauce* and *faucet*, the /le/ in *dawdle*, the ‹y› in *laundry* and *strawberry*, the ‹tion› in *audition*, the ‹ur› in *auburn*, the ‹age› saying /ij/ in *sausage*, and the suffixes ‹-ful› and ‹-some› in *awful* and *awesome*. Emphasize the ‹ar› in *awkward*.
- It may help the students to remember which alternative spelling to use if the words are put together in a silly sentence.
- It is a good idea to blend and sound out the spelling words quickly every day with the students.

Spelling List
jaw
hawk
sauce
haul
thaw
awful
flaw
dawdle
drawn
faucet
launch
laundry
awesome
audition
auburn
sausage
awkward
strawberry

Find the words from the spelling list. Which one is missing?

Look up each word in the dictionary and read its definition. Write the page number in the clean laundry.

Split these words into syllables.
awkward   autumn   lawnmower   awesome   astronaut

Parse these sentences and identify the subject in each one.

The large audience applauded loudly.

The barn owl hooted tiredly and yawned at the dawn.

50

Activity Page
- The students find the words from the spelling list in the word search and work out which is missing (*thaw*).
- Next, they use a dictionary to look up the words in the laundry. They read each definition and write the page numbers in the boxes. The students could also write a few sentences using some of the words.
- Then they identify the vowel sounds in the words and separate the words into syllables (*awk/ward, au/tumn, lawn/mow/er, awe/some, as/tro/naut*).
- Lastly they parse the sentences and identify the subject in each one (*audience, owl*). In the second sentence, *barn* is a noun acting as an adjective and should be underlined in blue.
  The <u>large</u> <u>audience</u> <u>applauded</u> <u>loudly</u>.
  The <u>barn</u> <u>owl</u> <u>hooted</u> <u>tiredly</u> <u>and</u> <u>yawned</u> <u>at</u> the <u>dawn</u>.

Dictation
Dictate the sentences below. Remind the class to use the correct punctuation in the first and second sentences. *August* and *Sam* are proper nouns and need capital letters.

1. Do you recall the awesome storm last August?
2. "I like strawberry sauce on my ice cream," commented Sam.
3. The lions and tigers have big claws.

Grammar: The Subject of a Sentence

Aim
- Refine the students' understanding of a sentence and develop their ability to identify its subject.

Introduction
- Review sentences. Write the following on the board without using a capital letter or period: *the farmer grows vegetables in*.
- Choose one of the students to read it out. Ask whether it is a sentence. Ask what is needed to make it a proper sentence (it needs to make sense, start with a capital letter, and end with the correct punctuation, in this case a period, but in others it could be a question mark or an exclamation mark).
- Add the capital letter, and ask how the sentence could be completed. Write one of the suggestions on the board and put a period at the end.
- Now write *The giant orange pumpkin.* on the board (with a capital letter and a period at the end). Ask why this is not a sentence (it does not have a verb).
- Ask the students to think of some ways to complete the sentence, identifying the verb in each one.

Main Point
- Tell the students that, as well as a verb, every sentence must have a subject. The subject of a sentence is the person, place, or thing that is doing or being what the verb describes.
- Look at the first sentence on the board (about the farmer) and identify the verb (*grows*), underlining it in red. Ask the students *Who or what grows the vegetables?* Draw a box around the word *farmer* and put a small ‹s› in one corner.
- Now replace *the farmer* with the pronoun *He* and ask which word is the subject now. Explain that the subject of a sentence is always a noun or pronoun.
- Look at the sentence about the pumpkin and identify the verb. For example, if the sentence were *The giant orange pumpkin grew to the size of a house*, you would underline the verb *grew* in red and ask the students *Who or what grew to the size of a house?*
- Draw a box around the word *pumpkin* and put a small ‹s› in the corner. Now write the following pair of sentences on the board and, with the students, find the verb and subject in each one:
  The black cat (subject) *chased* (verb) *the little mouse.*
  The little mouse (subject) *chased* (verb) *the black cat.*
- In answer to the question *Who or what chased the little mouse?* the students may reply *the black cat*. This is not wrong, but make sure you only draw a box around the noun *cat* and not any adjectives or articles that go with it.

- This is sometimes known as the "simple" subject.

Activity Page
- The students read each sentence, identify the verb, and underline it in red. They must remember to underline all the parts of the verb (e.g. *will be visiting* and *was swimming*).
- Then they identify the subject of the sentence by deciding who (or what) is "doing" or "being" the verb. They draw a box around the subject and put a small ‹s› in the corner.
- The subjects are as follows:
1. *birds*, 2. *Sam*, 3. *man*, 4. *cat*, 5. *Sophie*, 6. *rancher*, 7. *She*, 8. *vase*, 9. *You*, 10. *wind*, 11. *Ann*, 12. *rattlesnake*, 13. *I*, 14. *Sue*, 15. *kitten*, 16. *seal*.

Extension Activity
- The students write some sentences of their own and identify the verb and subject in each one.

Finishing the Lesson
- Look at the page with the students, checking their answers.
- If they have written their own sentences, ask some of the students to read them out and identify the verb and subject in each one.

Spelling: The ‹ie› Spelling of the /ee/ Sound

Spelling Test
- The students turn to the backs of their books and find the column labeled *Spelling Test 25*.
- In any order, call out the spelling words learned last week. The students write the words on the lines.

Review
- Write the following words on the board and blend and sound them out with the class: *snee**ze**, **no**se, pu**zzle**, b**ath**, **a**corn, **e**mail, **i**con, **o**val, her**o**, t**u**na.*
- Identify the various spelling patterns: ‹ze› and ‹s› saying /z/, ‹le› saying /ool/, ‹a› saying /ar/, and the vowel letters ‹a›, ‹e›, ‹i›, ‹o›, ‹u› saying their long sounds.

Spelling Point
- Remind the students that they know several ways to write the /ee/ sound, and ask them what they are: ‹ee›, ‹ea›, ‹e_e›, ‹y›, ‹ey›, ‹ie›, ‹e›.
- Explain that most words with an /ee/ sound take the ‹ee› or ‹ea› spellings (e.g. *seen, bean*). Although sometimes just ‹e› is used (e.g. *he, she*). When the /ee/ sound is at the end of a word, it is often spelled ‹ey› or ‹y› (e.g. *key, angry*) and, if the word is long or complicated, it might be spelled ‹e_e› (e.g. *complete*).
- Write *shriek* on the board and ask the class what sound the ‹ie› is making. Sound it out slowly with the students, /sh-r-ee-k/, and remind them that in some words, the letters ‹ie› make the /ee/ sound rather than the usual /ie/ sound.
- Write some more words on the board (e.g. *thief, belief, niece*), and blend and sound them out with the class, identifying the ‹ie› saying /ee/ in each word.

Spelling List
- Read the spelling words with the class and identify the ‹ie› making an /ee/ sound in each one. The students highlight the ‹ie› and put the long vowel mark over it. Explain the meanings of any unfamiliar words.
- Point out the soft ‹c› in *piece*, the ‹ze› in *frieze*, the silent ‹e› in *believe* and *achieve*, the ‹s› saying /z/ and ‹el› in *diesel*, the irregular plural in *thieves*, the soft ‹g› in *besiege*, the ‹au› and soft ‹c› in *audience*, the prefix ‹un-› and suffix ‹-able› in *unbelievable*.
- It may help the students to remember the ‹ie› spelling of /ee/ if they put together a silly sentence, using as many of the words as possible.

| field |
| chief |
| piece |
| brief |
| shield |
| grief |
| relief |
| frieze |
| fielder |
| priest |
| believe |
| achieve |
| diesel |
| thieves |
| besiege |
| audience |
| briefcase |
| unbelievable |

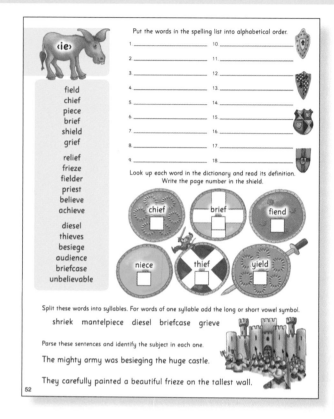

Activity Page
- The students put the spelling list words into alphabetical order (*achieve, audience, believe, besiege, brief, briefcase, chief, diesel, field, fielder, frieze, grief, piece, priest, relief, shield, thieves, unbelievable*).
- Next, the students use a dictionary to look up the words in the shields. They read each definition and write the page numbers in the boxes.
- Then they identify the vowel sounds in the words, separate the words into syllables (*man/tel/piece, die/sel, brief/case*), and put the long vowel mark over the ‹ie› in *shriek* and *grieve*.
- Finally, the students parse the sentences and identify the subject in each one (*army, They*). The first sentence is written in the past continuous, so both parts of the verb should be underlined in red.
  The <u>mighty</u> <u>army</u> <u>was besieging</u> the <u>huge</u> <u>castle</u>.
  <u>They</u> <u>carefully</u> <u>painted</u> a <u>beautiful</u> <u>frieze</u> <u>on</u> the <u>tallest</u> <u>wall</u>.

Dictation
- Dictate the sentences below. Remind the class to use the correct punctuation in the first sentence. *Saturday* is a proper noun and needs a capital letter.

> 1. "I think he is a thief," she shouted.
> 2. My niece and I will be shopping on Saturday.
> 3. They shrieked as the bull charged across the field.

Grammar: The Object of a Sentence

Aim
- Refine the students' understanding of a sentence. Develop their ability to identify both the subject and the object of a sentence.

Introduction
- Review sentences and remind the students that a sentence must start with a capital letter, contain a verb, make sense, and end with a period, a question mark, or an exclamation mark.
- Write on the board, *The farmer grows vegetables*.
- Choose one of the students to read it out and ask whether it is a sentence. (It is.)
- Remind them that a sentence also has to have a subject, that is, the noun or pronoun that is "doing" or "being" the verb.
- Ask the students to identify the verb (*grows*) and underline it in red.
- Now ask, *Who or what grows the vegetables?* (i.e. ask them for the subject of the sentence). Draw a box around *farmer* and put a small ‹s› in the corner.
- Write some more simple sentences on the board and identify the verb and subject in each one.

The Object of a Sentence

In each sentence, underline the verb(s) in red. Then find the subject and the object of the sentence. Put a box with a small ‹s› around the subject and a ring with a small ‹o› around the object.

The cat chased a mouse.

The rancher lassoed the cow.

I made a cake today.

Seth kicked the ball.

The lady wrote a letter.

The boy is reading a comic.

The artist painted a portrait.

The dog ate the bone.

He shut the drawer.

Megan opened the door.

Grandma knitted a scarf.

We prepared the salad for lunch.

She plays the flute beautifully.

Joe chased the puppy.

The puppy chased Joe.

I shall be learning a poem for the concert.

When you've finished, help Snake and me to color the picture.

Main Point
- As well as having a subject, a sentence may also have an object. Both the subject and object can be a person, place, or thing, but the subject "does" the verb action, and the object "receives" the verb action.
- Look at the sentence on the board and ask the students what they think the object of the sentence might be. Explain that they know what the subject and verb are (*farmer* and *grows* respectively). They can find the object by asking, *The farmer grows what?* Draw a ring around the word *vegetables* and put a small ‹o› inside.
- Now replace *vegetables* with the pronoun *them* and ask which word is the object now. Explain that, like the subject, the object of a sentence is always a noun or pronoun.
- Now write the following sentences on the board and, with the students, find the verb, subject, and object in each one:
  The black cat (subject) *chased* (verb) *the little mouse* (object).
  The little mouse (subject) *chased* (verb) *the black cat* (object).
- When the students are asked, *The black cat chased what?* to find the object of the first sentence, they may reply *the little mouse*. This is not wrong but make sure a ring is only drawn around the noun and not any adjectives or articles that go with it.

Activity Page
- The students read each sentence, identify the verb, and underline it in red. They must remember to underline all the parts of the verb (e.g. *is reading* and *will be learning*).
- Next, they identify the subject of the sentence by deciding who (or what) is "doing" or "being" the verb. They draw a box around the subject and put a small ‹s› in the corner.
- Then they decide who (or what) is "receiving" the verb action. They draw a ring around the object, with a small ‹o› inside.
- The subjects and objects are as follows:
  1. *cat* (S), *mouse* (O)
  2. *rancher* (S), *cow* (O)
  3. *I* (S), *cake* (O)
  4. *Seth* (S), *ball* (O)
  5. *lady* (S), *letter* (O)
  6. *boy* (S), *comic* (O)
  7. *artist* (S), *portrait* (O)
  8. *dog* (S), *bone* (O)
  9. *He* (S), *drawer* (O)
  10. *Megan* (S), *door* (O)
  11. *Grandma* (S), *scarf* (O)
  12. *We* (S), *salad* (O)
  13. *She* (S), *flute* (O)
  14. *Joe* (S), *puppy* (O)
  15. *puppy* (S), *Joe* (O)
  16. *I* (S), *poem* (O).

Extension Activity
- The students write some sentences of their own and identify the verb, subject, and object in each one.

Finishing the Lesson
- Read through the page with the students.

Spelling: The ⟨y⟩ Spelling of the /i/ Sound

Spelling Test

- The students turn to the backs of their books and find the column labeled *Spelling Test 26*.
- In any order, call out the spelling words learned last week. The students write the words on the lines.

Review

- Write the following words on the board and blend and sound them out with the class: *race, page, ask, chief, basic, equal, diet, poem, hello, duet*.
- Identify the various spelling patterns: soft ⟨c⟩ and ⟨g⟩, ⟨a⟩ saying /ar/, ⟨ie⟩ saying /ee/, and the vowel letters ⟨a⟩, ⟨e⟩, ⟨i⟩, ⟨o⟩, ⟨u⟩ saying their long sounds.

Spelling Point

- Remind the students that the letter ⟨y⟩ is a consonant that can also act as a vowel. It usually only makes the consonant sound /y/ when it comes at the beginning of a word (e.g. *yellow*). The rest of the time it is acting as a vowel, either as an alternative spelling of the /ie/ sound (e.g. *my, fly*) or as "toughy ⟨y⟩," replacing "shy ⟨i⟩" on the end of multisyllabic words like *fluffy, frosty,* and *happy*. Like any other vowel, it can use its "magic" to change a short vowel into a long vowel sound (e.g. *baby*).
- Explain that sometimes "toughy ⟨y⟩" replaces "shy ⟨i⟩" even if the /i/ sound is not at the end of a word (e.g. *gym, pyramid*). Point out that "toughy ⟨y⟩" at the end of a word is usually pronounced /ee/, but when it is inside a word, it keeps the /i/ sound.

Spelling List

- Read the spelling words with the class and identify the ⟨y⟩ making an /i/ sound in each one. The students highlight ⟨y⟩ and put the short vowel mark over it. Explain the meanings of any unfamiliar words. Point out the ⟨x⟩ and ⟨cs⟩ spellings of /ks/ in *lynx* and *lyrics*, the different spellings of /ool/ in *symbol, cymbal, typical, syllable,* and *physical*, the soft ⟨c⟩ in *cymbal*, the soft ⟨g⟩ in *Egypt*, the ⟨y⟩ saying /ee/ in *sympathy* and *mystery*, the silent ⟨h⟩ in *rhythm*, and the ⟨ph⟩ spelling and the ⟨s⟩ saying /z/ in *physical*. Compare the homophones *symbol* and *cymbal*, and remind the students that *Egypt* is a proper noun and needs a capital letter. It may help the students to remember the ⟨y⟩ spelling of /i/ if they put together a silly sentence.

abyss
myth
lynx
lyrics
syrup
idyllic
pyramid
symbol
cymbal
system
Egypt
typical
syllable
sympathy
mystery
rhythm
acrylic
physical

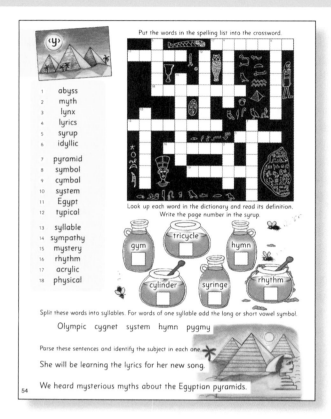

Activity Page

- The students fill in the crossword using the words from the spelling list. (The numbers in the crossword indicate the correct word from the spelling list.)
- Next, the students use a dictionary to look up the words in the syrup. They read each definition and write the page numbers in the boxes.
- Then they identify the vowel sounds in the words and separate the words into syllables (*o/lym/pic, cyg/net, sys/tem, pyg/my*) and put the short vowel mark over the ⟨y⟩ in *hymn*.
- Finally, the students parse the sentence and identify the subject in each one (*She, We*). The first sentence is written in the future continuous, so all parts of the verb should be underlined in red.

  She will be learning the lyrics for her new song.
  We heard mysterious myths about the Egyptian pyramids.

Dictation

- Dictate the sentences below. Remind the class to use the correct punctuation in the second sentence. *Nick* is a proper noun and needs a capital letter.

  1. He was given a new bicycle.
  2. "I will be using the new gym when it opens," enthused Nick.
  3. The secret code had symbols instead of letters.

Grammar: Subject and Object Pronouns

Aim
- Refine the students' understanding of pronouns and how they can change, depending on whether they are the subject or object of a sentence.

Introduction
- Remind the students that all sentences must have a subject, and that they can also have an object.
- Write the following sentences on the board:
  Tim (S) hit the cymbal (O).
  Seth (S) sang a song (O).
  Ann (S) met a famous actress (O).
  My brother (S) visited some friends (O) in Egypt.
  Some friends (S) visited my brother (O) in Egypt.
- With the students, identify the verb in each sentence. Next, decide who (or what) is "doing" the verb action and draw a box around the subject, with a small ‹s› in the corner. Then decide who or what is "receiving" the verb action and draw a ring around the object, with a small ‹o› inside.

Main Point
- Briefly review pronouns (*I, you, he/she/it, we, you, they*). Pronouns are short words that replace nouns and the color for them is pink.
- Write *I chased the dog* on the board and identify the verb (*chased*), subject (*I*), and object (*dog*).
- Remind the students that the subject and object of a sentence is always a noun or pronoun.
- Conjugate the sentence with the students (*I chased the dog, you chased the dog, he/she/it chased the dog,* and so on), doing the pronoun actions (page 9 of this *Teacher's Book*).
- Point out that the pronoun, which is the subject of the sentences, is different every time. Write each of the (subject) pronouns on the board.
- Now ask the students to change the sentence so that *dog* is the subject and *I* is the object. They should be able to hear that *The dog chased I* does not sound right, even if they do not know why.
- Write *The dog chased **me*** on the board and identify the different parts of the sentence. Ask the students what has changed.
- Explain that the pronoun *I*, which is the subject of the first sentence on the board, has changed to *me* now that it is the object of the second sentence.
- Now say, *You chased the dog. The dog chased…* and ask the students how to finish the second sentence (*you*). Do this for all of the pronouns and write the object pronouns (*me, you, him/her/it, us, you, them*) on the board. Discuss what has changed, or not changed, each time.

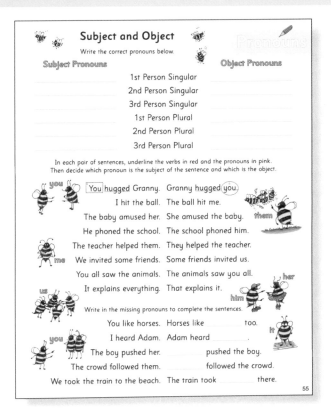

Activity Page
- The students write down the pronouns they would use for the subject of a sentence (*I, you, he/she/it, we, you, they*) and the pronouns they would use for the object of a sentence (*me, you, him/her/it, us, you, them*).
- Next, in the sentences below, they identify and underline the verbs in red and the pronouns in pink.
- The students then decide which pronoun is the subject and which is the object. They draw a box around the subject pronoun, with a small ‹s› in the corner, and draw a ring around the object pronoun, with a small ‹o› inside.
- Finally, the students read the pairs of sentences at the bottom of the page. They decide which pronouns are missing and write them in (*you, me, She, They, us*). It will help them if they identify the pronoun in the first sentence and write its corresponding subject or object pronoun in the second sentence.

Extension Activity
- The students choose pairs of pronouns (e.g. *I/me, he/him*) and use them in some sentence pairs.

Finishing the Lesson
- Look at the page with the students, checking their answers.

Spelling: The ‹a› Spelling of the /o/ Sound

Spelling Test
- The students turn to the backs of their books and find the column labeled *Spelling Test 27*.
- In any order, call out the spelling words learned last week. The students write the words on the lines.

Review
- Write the following words on the board and blend and sound them out with the class: *request, cast, field, system, crazy, legal, quiet, total, echo, menu.*
- Identify the spelling patterns: ‹qu› saying /kw/, ‹aw› saying /o/, ‹ie› saying /ee/, ‹y› saying /i/, and the vowel letters ‹a›, ‹e›, ‹i›, ‹o›, ‹u› saying their long sounds.

Spelling Point
- Write the words *wobble* and *swan* on the board and ask which letters are making the /wo/ sounds in each word. Sound the words out slowly with the class and underline ‹wo› in *wobble* and ‹wa› in *swan*.
- Remind the students that although some words with a /wo/ sound take the ‹wo› spelling, there are many that take the ‹wa› spelling. Ask the class for some suggestions and write them on the board (e.g. *wash, was, watch, wand, wasp*).
- Explain that it is really the sound /w/ that is changing the ‹a›. This is obvious in words with the ‹wa› spelling, but is also true of words that take the ‹qu› spelling.
- Write *squash* on the board and sound it out slowly with the students, /s-k-w-o-sh/. Remind the students that ‹qu› is really the two sounds /k/ and /w/ blended together and so the sound /w/ in ‹qu› is changing the sound of ‹a› into /o/.

Spelling List
- Read the spelling words with the class and identify the ‹a› making an /o/ sound in each one. The students highlight ‹a› and put the short vowel mark over it.
- Explain the meanings of any unfamiliar words.
- Emphasize the ‹et› in *wallet* and the ‹ar› in *quandary*.
- Point out the ‹tch› in *swatch* and *wristwatch*, the /le/ in *waddle*, *squabble*, and *twaddle*, the ‹y› in *wallaby*, *quandary*, and *quantity*, the silent ‹w› in *wristwatch*, and the ‹tion› in *qualification*.

Activity Page
- The students find the words from

swap
waft
swamp
wand
wallet
squad
swatch
squat
squalid
quality
wallaby
waddle
squabble
twaddle
quandary
wristwatch
quantity
qualification

the spelling list in the word search and work out which word is missing (*qualification*).
- Next, they use a dictionary to look up the words in the swans. They read each definition and write the page numbers in the boxes.
- Then they identify the vowel sounds in the words, separate the words into syllables (*quar/ry, wan/der, wal/let, twad/dle*) and put the short vowel mark over the ‹a› in *squash*.
- Finally, they parse the sentences and identify the subject in each one (*swallow, swan*). The second sentence is written in the present continuous, so both parts of the verb should be underlined in red. *River Thames* is a proper noun, so both *River* and *Thames* should be underlined in black.
  The swallow swoops high into the sunny sky.
  The white swan is floating gracefully along the River Thames.

Dictation
- Dictate the sentences below. Remind the class to use the correct punctuation in the first sentence. *Dutch* is a proper adjective and needs a capital letter.

1. "Look at the white swan," called the child.
2. They are watching a tennis match against a Dutch team.
3. The wasps buzzed around the fizzy drinks.

Grammar: *Possessive Pronouns*

Aim
- Refine the students' understanding of personal pronouns and introduce the possessive pronouns.

Introduction
- Briefly review pronouns and their actions (see page 9). These are called personal pronouns.
- Remind the students that personal pronouns can change depending on whether the noun they are replacing is the subject of a sentence (*I, you, he/she/ it, we, you, they*) or the object (*me, you, him/her/it, us, you, them*). For example, in the sentence *John saw Sue*, the subject *John* can be replaced by *he* to make *He saw Sue*. However, if the sentence were changed to *Sue saw John*, *John* would be the object and could be replaced by *him*.
- Now review the possessive adjectives (*my, your, his/her/its, our, your, their*). Possessive adjectives describe a noun by saying who it belongs to. Instead of saying *It is Ben's pen,* we can say *It is his pen.*
- Point out that because the word *his* is used instead of *Ben's* it acts in a similar way to pronouns.
- Remind the students that there is one possessive adjective for each of the pronouns (*I/my, you/your, he/his, she/her, it/its, we/our, you/your, they/their*).

Main Point
- Tell the students you are going to write some sentences using some of the pronouns and possessive adjectives learned so far.
- Write the following three sentences on the board: *I have a pen. The pen belongs to me. It is my pen.*
- With the students, identify the personal pronouns (*I, me*) and the possessive adjective (*my*). Point out that each sentence gives the same information in a different way. Look at the last sentence again and ask the students if the sentence can be made even shorter. Ask the students what word they could use instead of *my pen*.
- Write *It is mine* on the board and explain that the word *mine* is a possessive pronoun. It is a pronoun because it is a short word that replaces the noun *pen*, and it is "possessive" because it says who the pen belongs to. Underline the word *mine* in pink.
- Write three more sentences on the board: *You have a book. The book belongs to you. It is your book.*
- With the students, identify the personal pronouns (*you, you*) and the possessive adjective (*your*).
- Write *It is* on the board and ask the students whether they know the possessive pronoun. Write in *yours*, underlining it in pink.
- Make up some more sentences to introduce the other possessive pronouns (*hers/his/its, ours, yours,*

theirs), underlining each one in pink. Tell the students that, unlike the personal pronouns, the possessive pronouns do not change when they are the object of a sentence. The pronoun actions can be used to practice the pronouns and possessive adjectives learned so far. (It is important the students remember that although possessive adjectives act in a similar way to pronouns, they are still adjectives.)

Subject Pronouns	Object Pronouns	Possessive Adjectives	Possessive Pronouns
I	me	my	mine
you	you	your	yours
he/she/it	him/her/it	his/her/its	his/hers/its
we	us	our	ours
you	you	your	yours
they	them	their	theirs

Activity Page
- The students read each pair of sentences and write a new sentence underneath. They should start with *It is* and complete the sentence by writing the appropriate possessive pronoun, underlining it in pink.

Extension Activity
- The students reread the sentences, and underline the personal pronouns in pink and the possessive adjectives in blue.

Spelling: The ‹al› Spelling of the /o/ Sound

Spelling Test
- The students turn to the backs of their books and find the column labeled *Spelling Test 28.*
- In any order, call out the spelling words learned last week. The students write the words on the lines.

Review
- Write the following words on the board and blend and sound them out with the class: *launch, thief, lyrics, swap, haste, regal, idea, okay, zero, tulip.*
- Identify the spelling patterns: ‹au› saying /o/, ‹ie› saying /ee/, ‹y› saying /i/, ‹a› saying /o/, and the vowel letters ‹a›, ‹e›, ‹i›, ‹o›, ‹u› saying their long sounds.

Spelling Point
- Review the main ways of writing the /o/ sound and write them on the board: ‹o›, ‹aw›, ‹au›, ‹al›.
- Ask the students to suggest words for each alternative spelling. As each word is called out, ask the students which spelling it takes and write it under the appropriate heading. Examples of possible words can be found on page 80 of this book.
- Point out that in some ‹al› words, the letter ‹l› is also pronounced (e.g. *halt, salt*).

Spelling List
- Remind the students that they have looked at words with the ‹aw› and ‹au› spellings (see page 80). This time, they are going to look at words with ‹al›.
- Read the spelling words with the students and identify the ‹al› making the /o/ sound in each one. The students highlight the letters making the /o/ sound.
- Explain the meanings of any unfamiliar words.
- Point out the ‹o› saying /oa/ in *also*, the ‹se› saying /s/ in *false*, the ‹ea› saying /e/ in *already*, and the ‹w› making the ‹a› say /o/ in *waterfall.*
- Also look at how the ‹l› in *halt, also, alter, salt, almost, walrus, false, already, alternative, altogether,* and *alteration* is part of the ‹al› spelling, but also says its own sound.
- It may help the students to remember the ‹al› spelling of /o/ if they put together a silly sentence, using as many of the words as possible.
- It is a good idea to blend and sound out the spelling words quickly every day with the class.

halt
also
talk
alter
mall
salt
almost
fallen
walrus
false
recall
already
eyeball
waterfall
alternative
baseball
altogether
alteration

Which words in the spelling list match these descriptions?

1. _____ (it can be added to food)
2. _____ (very nearly, but not quite)
3. _____ (another option)
4. _____ (a sea animal with tusks)
5. _____ (to remember something)
6. _____ (not real, or untrue)
7. _____ (to stop moving suddenly)
8. _____ (as well, too)
9. _____ (a covered shopping center)
10. _____ (a change in something)

Look up each word in the dictionary and read its definition. Write the page number in the basketball.

stalk   altar   false   overalls   bald   walk

Split these words into syllables. For words of one syllable add the long or short vowel symbol.

install   already   beanstalk   walrus   sidewalk

Parse these sentences and identify the subject in each one.

Jack climbed the giant beanstalk.

The boys played baseball near the mall.

58

Activity Page
- The students read the phrases and decide which words from the spelling list they describe.
- Next, they use a dictionary to look up the words in the basketballs. They read each definition and write the page numbers in the boxes.
- Then they identify the vowel sounds in the words and separate the words into syllables (*in/stall, al/read/y, bean/stalk, wal/rus, side/walk*).
- Finally, they parse the sentences and identify the subject in each one (*Jack, boys*).

Jack climbed the giant beanstalk.

The boys played baseball near the mall.

Dictation
- Dictate the sentences below. Remind the class to use the correct punctuation in the second sentence.

1. We also played football after school.
2. "The bald pirate had a false leg," explained the boy.
3. They almost halted the talk about baseball.

Grammar: Homophones ("Our" and "Are")

Aim
· Refine the students' understanding of homophones and develop their ability to choose between similar-sounding words like *our* and *are* in their writing.

Introduction
· Review the possessive adjectives (*my, your, his/her/ its, our, your, their*) and possessive pronouns (*mine, yours, his/hers/its, ours, yours, theirs*). Ask the students to use some of them in sentences.
· Review the irregular verb *to be* and conjugate it with the students, using the pronoun actions (see page 9).

Main Point
· Remind the students that it is important to be careful when writing the words *our* and *are* as they sometimes sound similar when they are spoken in a sentence.
· The word *our* is more properly pronounced /ou-r/ but in practice it is often pronounced /ar/. Emphasize the correct pronunciation for each word when you are talking about them to help the students remember the difference.
· On the board, write *We are putting our books on the table*. Discuss the different spellings and meanings of *our* and *are* with the students.
· Point out that the word *are* is part of the verb *to be* (it is being used here as the auxiliary verb in the present continuous tense of the verb *to put*).
· *Our* is a possessive adjective, which is describing the books by saying who owns them.
· Remind the class that words that sound similar to one another but have different spellings and meanings are called *homophones*. It is very important for the students to use the correct homophone in their writing, otherwise it will not make sense. They need to stop and think before writing the word, decide which meaning is needed, and think how the word with that meaning is spelled.
· Write the following sentences on the board, leaving a space for *our* and *are*, and ask the students which word is needed to complete each one:
We put on (our) coats to play outside.
We (are) going to play outside.
· Remind the class to think about what kind of word is missing (should it be an adjective or a verb?) to help them choose the correct one.
· Ask the students to suggest some sentences using *our* and *are*, write them on the board, and discuss which word is needed in each one.

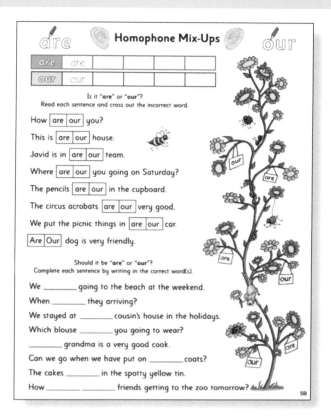

Activity Page
· The students write inside the outlined words *our* and *are* at the top of the page and practice writing the words in the table.
· Next, they read the sentences, decide which is the correct word, and cross out the wrong one.
· Then they read the sentences at the bottom of the page, decide which word is needed to complete each one, and write it on the line. In the last sentence, the students need to use both *are* (first) and *our* (second).

Extension Activity
· The students think up some sentences of their own using *our* or *are* and write them down.
· Alternatively, the students can work in pairs, taking it in turns to dictate a sentence using *our* or *are* for their partner to write. Together they decide whether the correct word has been used.

Finishing the Lesson
· Look at the page with the students, checking their answers.
· If they have written their own sentences, ask some of the students to read them out and identify whether they have used *our* or *are*.

Spelling: Homophones

Spelling Test
- The students turn to the backs of their books and find the column labeled *Spelling Test 29.*
- Call out the spelling words learned last week.

Review
- Write the following words on the board and blend and sound them out with the class: *syrup, waft, draw, haul, walk, maple, secret, wild, only, music.*
- Identify the spelling patterns: ‹y› saying /i/, ‹a› saying /o/, ‹aw›, ‹au›, and ‹al› saying /o/, and the vowel letters ‹a›, ‹e›, ‹i›, ‹o›, ‹u› saying their long sounds.

Spelling Point
- Remind the students that homophones are words that sound similar to one another but have different spellings and meanings. Explain that it is very important for the students to use the correct word in their writing, otherwise it will not make sense.
- Review the homophones *to, too,* and *two, for* and *four,* and *are* and *our.* (*Are* and *our* are not strictly homophones, but in some regions they sound the same or very similar and it is useful for the students to be aware of this.)
- Write some sentences on the board using these words, or ask the students for their suggestions. Decide with the class which word should be used in each sentence. For example, *I went (to) town today. I have (two) pets. I would like some more, (too). I went (for) a walk. (Four) of us walked into town. Here (are) the cups. This is (our) house.*
- See whether the students can think of any other homophones (e.g. *beech/beach, see/sea, flour/flower, right/write, wait/weight, whole/hole, meet/meat, hear/here, cymbal/symbol*). Remind them that if they are unsure which word to use, they can check the spellings and meanings in a dictionary.

Spelling List
- Read the spelling words with the students and identify the pairs of homophones. Discuss the different meanings and spellings with the class, and explain the meanings of any unfamiliar words.
- Point out the ‹ue› and ‹ew› spellings of the long /oo/ sound in *blue* and *blew,* the ‹eigh› saying /ai/ in *eight,* the ‹ea› saying /e/ in *weather,* and the silent ‹h› in *whether.*

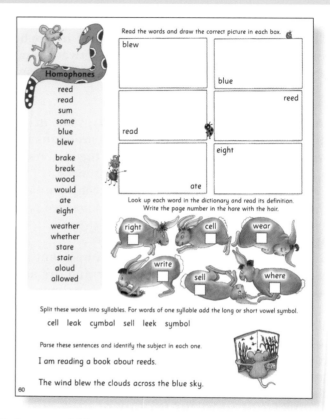

reed
read
sum
some
blue
blew
brake
break
wood
would
ate
eight
weather
whether
stare
stair
aloud
allowed

- It is a good idea to blend and sound out the spelling words quickly every day.

Activity Page
- The students read each word and illustrate it.
- Next, they use a dictionary to look up the words in the hares with the hair. They read each definition and write the page numbers in the boxes.
- They separate the words into syllables (*cym/bal, sym/bol*) and put short vowel marks over the ‹e› in *cell* and *sell,* and long vowel marks over the ‹ea› and ‹ee› in *leak* and *leek.*
- Finally, they parse the sentences and identify the subject in each one (*I, wind*). The first sentence is written in the present continuous so both parts of the verb should be underlined in red.
  I am reading a book about reeds.
  The wind blew the clouds across the blue sky.

Dictation
- Dictate the sentences below. Remind the class to use the correct punctuation in the second and third sentences. *Tim* is a proper noun and needs a capital letter.

1. I hope I write the right words.
2. "I can see the sea," shouted the children excitedly.
3. "I would like to go to the wood," declared Tim.

Grammar: Homophones *("There," "Their," and "They're")*

Aim
- Refine the students' knowledge of the homophones *there, their,* and *they're,* and the differences in their meanings and spellings. Develop the students' ability to choose between these homophones in their writing.

Introduction
- Review homophones. Homophones are words that sound similar to one another, but have different spellings and meanings.
- Review the words *our* and *are,* which can sometimes sound the same or very similar.
- Remind the students that it is very important they use the correct word in their writing, otherwise it will not make sense. To help them make the right choice, the students must think about what kind of word is needed (e.g. *our* is a possessive adjective that describes a noun, but *are* is part of the verb *to be*).
- Ask the students to suggest a sentence for each word.

Main Point
- The homophones *there, their,* and *they're* are also commonly confused in writing.
- Write the words on the board and discuss each one in turn. *There* is often used to introduce the subject of a sentence, as in *There is a bird in the tree,* or to show position, as in *Put it over there* (when it is acting as an adverb).
- The word *their* is a possessive adjective, as in *They put on their hats.* Like the other possessive adjectives (*my, your, his/her/its, our, your*) it describes a noun by saying who it belongs to.
- *They're* is a contraction of *they are,* which is part of the verb *to be.* The apostrophe has replaced the ‹a› in *are* and the two words have been joined together. Explain that if the students can replace the homophone with *they are* in a sentence, as in *They're (They are) going to the park later,* and it still makes sense, they know to use *they're.* Remind the students that contractions are mostly used in speech or when writing a friendly note.
- Write the following sentences on the board, leaving a space for *there, their,* and *they're,* and ask the students which word is needed to complete each one:
  They put on (their) coats to play outside.
  (They're) going to play outside.
  They will be playing over (there).
- The students need to think about what kind of word is missing to help them choose the correct one. Is the word they need describing a noun by saying who it belongs to; is it replacing *they are;* is it introducing the subject of the sentence or showing position?

- Ask the students to suggest some sentences using *there, their,* or *they're.* Write them on the board, and discuss which word is needed in each one.

Activity Page
- The students write inside the outlined words *there, their,* and *they're* at the top of the page and practice writing the words on the lines.
- Next, they read the sentences, decide which is the correct word and cross out the wrong ones.
- Then they read the sentences at the bottom of the page, decide which word is needed to complete each one and write it on the line. In the last sentence, the students need to use *there* (first), *their* (second), and *they're* (third).

Extension Activity
- The students think up some sentences of their own using *there, their,* or *they're* and write them down.
- Alternatively, the students can work in pairs, taking it in turns to dictate a sentence using *there, their,* or *they're* for their partner to write. Together they decide whether the correct word has been used.

Finishing the Lesson
- Look at the page with the students, checking their answers.

Spelling: ‹ear›, ‹eer›, and ‹ere›

Spelling Test
- The students turn to the backs of their books and find the column labeled *Spelling Test 30*.
- In any order, call out the spelling words learned last week. The students write the words on the lines.

Review
- Write the following words on the board and blend and sound them out with the class: *brief, myth, law, fault, stalk, our, are, there, their, they're*.
- Identify the spelling patterns: ‹ie› saying /ee/, ‹y› saying /i/, and ‹aw›, ‹au›, and ‹al› saying /o/.
- Discuss the different spellings and meanings of *our* and *are*, and *there, their,* and *they're*.

Spelling Point
- Write ‹ear› on the board and ask the students what it says. Remind them that, as well as being a word, /ear/ is a sound found in words like *near* and *year*. (It is sometimes thought of as two sounds: an /i/ sound running into an /er/ sound.)
- See whether the students can think of any other words with this spelling (e.g. *dear, tear, fear, spear*).
- They may remember that the ‹ear› spelling can also make the /air/ sound, as in *bear* and *pear*.
- Explain that although the majority of words take the ‹ear› spelling of the /ear/ sound, there are two other main ways it can be spelled: ‹eer› as in *beer, deer, jeer, cheer, sneer, steer, peer, career*, and ‹ere› as in *here, mere, interfere, sphere, adhere, severe*.
- Add ‹eer› and ‹ere› to the board and make a short list of words for each spelling. Blend and sound out the words with the class, identifying the ‹ear›, ‹eer›, or ‹ere› spelling in each one.

Spelling List
- Read the spelling words with the students and identify the letters making the /ear/ sound in each one. The students highlight the letters making the /ear/ sound.
- Explain the meanings of any unfamiliar words.
- Point out the compound word *gearbox*, the suffixes ‹-ful› and ‹-ing› in *fearful* and *sneering*, the prefix ‹dis-› in *disappear*, the soft ‹c› in *appearance*, and the ‹ph› in *atmosphere*.
- It may help the students to remember each spelling if words with the same spelling are put together in a silly sentence.

deer
hear
steer
peer
rear
cheer
here
clear
mere
gearbox
fearful
sneering
interfere
dreary
disappear
smeary
appearance
atmosphere

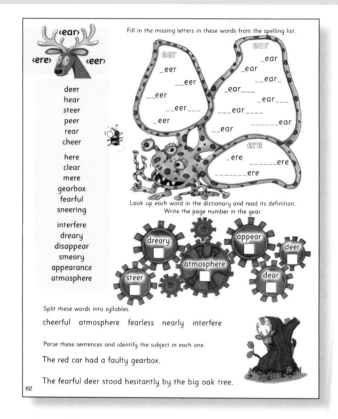

Activity Page
- The students complete the words from the spelling list (in the ears) by writing in the missing letters.
- Next, they use a dictionary to look up the words in the gears. They read each definition and write the page numbers in the boxes. The students could also write a few sentences using some of the words.
- Then they identify the vowel sounds in the words and separate the words into syllables (*cheer/ful, at/mo/sphere, fear/less, near/ly, in/ter/fere*).
- Finally, they parse the sentences and identify the subject in each one (*car, deer*). In the second sentence, *oak* is a noun acting as an adjective and should be underlined in blue.

The <u>red</u> <u>car</u> <u>had</u> a <u>faulty</u> <u>gearbox</u>.
The <u>fearful</u> <u>deer</u> <u>stood</u> <u>hesitantly</u> <u>by</u> the <u>big</u> <u>oak</u> <u>tree</u>.

Dictation
- Dictate the sentences below. Remind the class to use the correct punctuation in the second and third sentences. *Beth* and *Bill* are proper nouns and need capital letters.

1. The cheering crowd was waiting for the prince and princess's appearance.
2. "My best earrings have disappeared," said Beth.
3. "Did you hear the dreary speech?" asked Bill.

Grammar: Questions and Exclamations in Speech

Aim
- Refine the students' understanding of questions and exclamations.
- Develop the students' ability to use question marks and exclamation marks in written speech.

Introduction
- Review speech marks and how to use them.
- On the board, draw a head with a speech bubble coming out of its mouth (or find a similar picture in a comic or story book). Show it to the students and ask them what they think the person is saying. (e.g. *"I saw you," said Bill.*)
- Now ask the students how they would write this in a sentence.
- Remind them to start with opening speech marks ("66"), write what is being said (starting with a capital letter), then finish the speech with a comma and closing speech marks ("99"). They must also remember to say who is speaking and finish with a period.
- Point out that the sentence could begin the other way around, starting with the person speaking (e.g. *Bill said, "I saw you."*).
- Remind the class that in sentences like this one they must remember to put the comma outside the speech marks and put a period at the end of the speech. Say the sentence with the students and encourage them to act it out with you (see page 61).

Main Point
- Write *What is your name?* on the board and ask the students what is different about this sentence.
- They should be able to say that it is a question and it has a question mark at the end and not a period. They may also notice that it has one of the ‹wh› question words, *what*, which is being asked to get some information.
- Ask the students to suggest some more questions, using the other question words (*why, when, where, who, which, whose,* and *what*).
- Now write *Go away!* on the board and remind the students that this is called an exclamation. It has an exclamation mark at the end instead of a period. The exclamation mark is used to show that the speaker feels strongly about something.
- Ask the students whether they can think of any other exclamations (e.g. *Help! Wow! That hurt! I don't believe it!*) and write them on the board.
- Tell the students that you are going to write the question in a sentence. Start with opening speech marks ("66") and discuss what to do as you write it on the board. Explain that instead of putting a

comma at the end of the speech, they should write a question mark to show it is a question.
- They could also use the word *asked* instead of *said*. Encourage the students to think of other *asking* verbs they might use (e.g. *wondered, enquired, questioned*).
- Repeat the activity, this time with the exclamation. Point out that instead of putting a comma at the end of the speech, they should use an exclamation mark to show that the person speaking feels strongly.
- Encourage them to use an alternative word for *said* (e.g. *exclaimed, shouted, called, shrieked*).

Activity Page
- The students write inside the outlined question marks and exclamation marks at the top of the page.
- Then they look at each speech bubble and write what is being said in a sentence. They must remember to explain who is speaking, using the verb suggested, and to write in the correct punctuation. If it is a question, they write a question mark at the end of the speech, followed by closing speech marks ("99"). If it is an exclamation, they should write an exclamation mark.

Extension Activity
- Provide some comic books for the students. They look for questions or exclamations in speech bubbles, and write out the speech as sentences.

Spelling: ⟨ure⟩

Spelling Test
- The students turn to the backs of their books and find the column labeled *Spelling Test 31*.
- Call out the spelling words learned last week.

Review
- Write the following words on the board and blend and sound them out with the class: *yawn, audible, talk, hear, cheer, here, swamp, Egypt, piece, peace.*
- Identify the spelling patterns: ⟨aw⟩, ⟨au⟩, and ⟨al⟩ saying /o/, ⟨ear⟩, ⟨eer⟩, and ⟨ere⟩ saying /ear/, ⟨a⟩ saying /o/, ⟨y⟩ saying /i/, and ⟨ie⟩ saying /ee/.
- Discuss the different spellings and meanings of *here* and *hear,* and *piece* and *peace.*

Spelling Point
- Review the ⟨ture⟩ spelling. Remind the class that it is really made up of three sounds, /t-ue-r/, but at the end of multisyllabic words it often sounds like /cher/, as in *picture* and *nature.*
- Write *treasure* on the board and explain that ⟨ure⟩ does not always follow the letter ⟨t⟩. Many words end in ⟨sure⟩, where the ⟨s⟩ makes the /zh/ sound, but ⟨ure⟩ can be preceded by other letters as well. As with ⟨ture⟩, the /ue-r/ sound heard in *pure* and *cure* often becomes a schwa, or swallowed vowel, in multisyllabic words like *figure* and *conjure.*
- The ⟨ure⟩ spelling often varies in how it is pronounced, according to the letters that precede it.

Spelling List
- Read the spelling words with the students and identify the ⟨ure⟩ spelling in each one. Ask the class to highlight ⟨ure⟩ and look at the letter which comes before it. Explain the meanings of any unfamiliar words.
- Point out the ⟨ea⟩ in *feature*, the ⟨n⟩ saying /ng/ in *puncture*, the ⟨ss⟩ saying /sh/ in *pressure*, the ⟨s⟩ saying /zh/ in the other ⟨sure⟩ words, the ⟨ei⟩ in *leisure*, the ⟨ea⟩ saying /e/ in *pleasure, treasure,* and *measurement*, and the ⟨o⟩ saying /oa/ in *composure*. It may also help the students if they emphasize the /ue-r/ in each word.

capture
fixture
vulture
feature
puncture
moisture
pressure
leisure
pleasure
treasure
composure
measurement
figure
failure
conjure
mature
secure
manicure

Activity Page
- The students find the words from the spelling list in the word search and work out which word is missing (*puncture*).

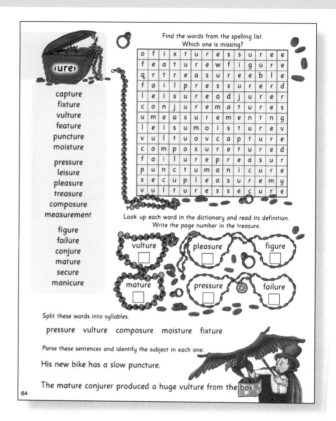

- Next, they use a dictionary to look up the words in the treasure. They read each definition and write the page numbers in the boxes. The students could also write a few sentences using some of the words.
- Then they identify the vowel sounds in the words and separate the words into syllables (*pres/sure, vul/ture, com/po/sure, mois/ture, fix/ture*).
- Finally, they parse the sentences and identify the subject in each one (*bike, conjurer*).
  His new bike has a slow puncture.
  The mature conjurer produced a huge vulture from the box.

Dictation
- Dictate the sentences below. Remind the class to use the correct punctuation in the second sentence. *Trevor* is a proper noun and needs a capital letter.

1. I fractured my arm while having an adventure.
2. "I took a picture of the creature!" exclaimed Trevor.
3. The pirates measured their treasure.

Extension Activity
- The students make a list of words with the ⟨ure⟩ spelling in their Spelling Word Books.

Grammar: *Prefixes*

Aim
- Refine the students' knowledge of prefixes and how they change the meaning of words.

Introduction
- Review suffixes. A suffix is usually one or more syllables added at the end of a word to change its meaning.
- Ask the students to think of some suffixes they know, such as ‹-ed›, ‹-less›, ‹-able›, and ‹-ful›. Remind them that if a suffix starts with a vowel letter, there will be some spelling rules for adding that suffix.
- Now remind the students that one or more syllables can also be added at the beginning of a word to change its meaning. Ask them what this is called (a prefix).
- Write *prefix* on the board and ask the students whether they know what the letters ‹pre-› usually mean in words like *prepare, prevent*, and *predict*. (If you are prepared, you are ready for something before it happens; if you prevent something, you stop it before it happens, and if you predict something, you guess it will happen before it does.)
- So, *prefix* has the prefix ‹pre-› meaning *before*. This tells the students that the letters in a prefix are added before the root word.
- Unlike suffixes, prefixes do not usually have any spelling rules for the students to remember.

Main Point
- Write the word *well* on the board and discuss what it means with the students.
- Now add the prefix ‹un-› to make *unwell* and ask them what the word means now. Ask the students for other examples (e.g. *happy/unhappy, successful/unsuccessful, kind/unkind*).
- Point out that the words starting with the prefix ‹un-› mean the opposite of the root words. So, ‹un-› means *not*. Ask one of the students to think of a sentence using *well* and another student to think of a sentence using *unwell*.
- Review the prefixes covered in the *Grammar 2 Student Book* in the same way, and discuss their meanings:
- ‹de-› and ‹dis-›, meaning *undo* or *remove* (e.g. *decode, devalue, disappear, disagree*)
- ‹mis-›, meaning *wrongly* or *not* (e.g. *misplace, mistake, misunderstand, mistrust*)
- ‹im-›, meaning *not* (e.g. *immature, impatient, impossible*)
- ‹non-›, meaning *not* (e.g. *nonstop, nonsense*)
- ‹re-›, meaning *again* (e.g. *recycle, refill, replace*)
- ‹mid-›, meaning *middle* (e.g. *midsummer, midnight*)
- ‹semi-›, meaning *half* (e.g. *semicircle, semifinal*)

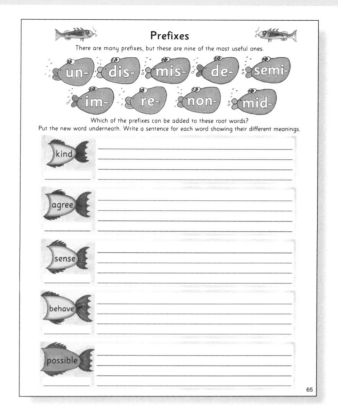

Activity Page
- The students look at each root word in turn and decide which prefix can be added to it to make a new word. They write the new word underneath.
- Then they write a sentence for each word (the original word and the new word) to show their different meanings.

Extension Activity
- Provide colored paper, pens, and scissors for the students to make their own "prefix fish." See the illustration on page 25 of this *Teacher's Book*.
- The students cut out nine fish head shapes and write a different prefix on each one: ‹un-›, ‹dis-›, ‹de-›, ‹mis-›, ‹semi-›, ‹im-›, ‹non-›, ‹re-›, ‹mid-›.
- Next, they cut out as many fish body shapes (with tails) as they can and write a different root word in each one. Good examples of root words include the following: *fair, safe, code, hydrate, appear, like, behave, place, circle, final, possible, polite, sense, stop, build, cycle, day, way.*
- The students use the fish pieces to make new words, deciding which of the prefixes on the heads can be added to the words on the fish bodies to make new adjectives.
- They could also copy the new words down and use some of them in sentences.

Spelling: The ‹gn› Spelling of the /n/ Sound

Spelling Test
- The students turn to the backs of their books and find the column labeled *Spelling Test 32.*
- In any order, call out the spelling words learned last week. The students write the words on the lines.

Review
- Write the following words on the board and blend and sound them out with the class: *dawn, sauce, salt, clear, sneer, interfere, write, right, flour, flower.*
- Identify the spelling patterns: ‹aw›, ‹au›, ‹al› saying /o/, and ‹ear›, ‹eer›, ‹ere›, saying /ear/.
- Discuss the different spellings and meanings of *write* and *right,* and *flour* and *flower.*

Spelling Point
- Remind the class that some words have silent letters.
- Write the following words on the board and ask the students to find the silent letters: *lamb, write, knight, hour, scent.*
- Explain that some silent letters often go with a particular letter, as in ‹mb› (*thumb, climb, comb*), ‹wr› (*wreck, write, wrap*), ‹kn› (*knee, knit, knock*), and ‹sc› (*scene, muscle, scissors*).
- Point out that the words sound the same with or without the silent letter. This makes them different from "magic ‹e›" words, because if a "magic ‹e›" is removed it changes the sound of the vowel (e.g. *cape* becomes *cap*). However, it is still important to remember the silent letters.
- Write *night, our,* and *sent* on the board and compare their meanings with *knight, hour,* and *scent.*
- Introduce the ‹gn› spelling of /n/. Write *gnat* on the board and ask the students which letter is silent.
- Write some words from the spelling list on the board or ask the students to suggest some other ‹gn› words.

Spelling List
- Read the spelling words with the students and identify the ‹gn› spelling in each one. Ask the class to highlight the ‹gn›.
- Explain the meanings of any unfamiliar words.
- Point out the ‹u› saying /oo/ in *gnu,* the ‹i› saying its long vowel sound in all the words with ‹ign› (aside from ‹eign› and ‹oign›), the ‹aw› in *gnaw,* the ‹o› saying /oa/ in *signpost,* and the ‹ei› in *reign, feign,* and

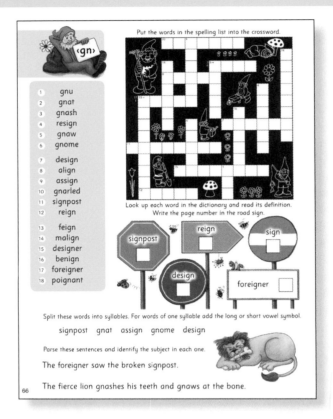

1	gnu
2	gnat
3	gnash
4	resign
5	gnaw
6	gnome
7	design
8	align
9	assign
10	gnarled
11	signpost
12	reign
13	feign
14	malign
15	designer
16	benign
17	foreigner
18	poignant

Put the words in the spelling list into the crossword.

Look up each word in the dictionary and read its definition. Write the page number in the road sign.

signpost   reign   sign   design   foreigner

Split these words into syllables. For words of one syllable add the long or short vowel symbol.

signpost   gnat   assign   gnome   design

Parse these sentences and identify the subject in each one.

The foreigner saw the broken signpost.

The fierce lion gnashes his teeth and gnaws at the bone.

66

foreigner. It may also help the students if they pronounce each silent ‹g› (e.g. /g/-nu, /g/-nashed).

Activity Page
- The students fill in the crossword using the words from the spelling list. (The numbers in the crossword indicate the correct word from the spelling list.)
- Next, they use a dictionary to look up the words in the signs. They read each definition and write the page numbers in the boxes. The students could also write a few sentences using some of the words.
- Then they identify the vowel sounds in the words, separate the words into syllables (*sign/post, as/sign, de/sign*), put a short vowel mark over the ‹a› in *gnat,* and a long vowel mark over the ‹o› in *gnome* (as well as a dot over the ‹e›). Finally, they parse the sentences and identify the subject in each one (*foreigner, lion*).
  The <u>foreigner</u> <u>saw</u> the <u>broken</u> <u>signpost</u>.
  The <u>fierce</u> <u>lion</u> <u>gnashes</u> <u>his</u> <u>teeth</u> <u>and</u> <u>gnaws</u> <u>at</u> the <u>bone</u>.

Dictation
- Dictate the sentences below. Remind the class to use the correct punctuation in the first sentence. *Ann* is a proper noun and needs a capital letter.

1. "Is that a designer dress?" enquired Ann.
2. The gnu flicked his tail at the gnats.
3. The old oak tree had a gnarled and twisted trunk.

Grammar: *Collective Nouns*

Aim
- Refine the students' knowledge of nouns and introduce collective nouns. Collective nouns are words that describe a group of objects: for example, *a **bunch** of flowers* or *a **herd** of elephants*.

Introduction
- Review nouns. Nouns are the names given to particular people, places, and dates (proper nouns) or generic "things" (common nouns). The color for all types of noun is black.
- Review the actions. (Proper nouns: the students touch their forehead with their index and middle fingers. Common nouns: the students touch their forehead with their hand.) Remind the students that a proper noun starts with a capital letter.
- Write *Anna and Tom went to Spain in August* on the board and identify all the proper nouns with the students, underlining them in black.
- Repeat this activity, only this time write some sentences with common nouns. Remind the students that the words *a* or *an* (the indefinite articles) or *the* (the definite article) can usually be put in front of a common noun (e.g. *We went for **a** walk in **the** park and saw **the** ducks. There was **an** egg in **the** nest*).

Main Point
- There are three types of common noun: concrete, abstract, and collective. So far, the students have learned about concrete nouns (things that they can see and touch).
- Explain to the students that they are going to learn about another type of noun called a collective noun. These are words that describe a group of objects. They could describe a group of people, animals, or things (or even a group of ideas or emotions, but these are abstract nouns, which will be introduced when the students are older).
- Write the following phrases on the board and ask the students to identify the nouns and the collective nouns in each: *a **class** of students, a **herd** of cows, a **pack** of cards*.
- Point out that the nouns *students, cows,* and *cards* are plural because there are many of them, but the collective nouns *class, herd,* and *pack* are singular because they describe the group as a whole.
- Ask the students whether they can think of any other collective nouns and write them on the board.
- It is important not to confuse collective nouns with uncountable nouns. Uncountable nouns (e.g. *water, meat, furniture*) are usually singular and cannot be divided into smaller groups of one particular item.

- Collective nouns can be plural and describe a group of one particular type of object (e.g. *one **pack** of cards, two **packs** of cards*).

Activity Page
- The students circle the collective noun in each sentence (*shoal, bunch, flock, fleet, colony, audience*) and underline it, and any other nouns, in black.
- Next, they complete each collective noun phrase with a suitable noun (e.g. *a choir of singers, a herd of cows, a bouquet of roses, a team of swimmers, a crowd of sightseers, a library of maps*).
- Finally, they look at the pictures at the bottom of the page and write the collective noun for each one: *flock* (of sheep), *bunch* (of bananas), *band* (of musicians).

Extension Activity
- The students complete the "Collective Noun Zoo" on page 80 of their *Student Books* by drawing a number of the appropriate animal in each area. (This can also be used as a "filler" activity for any spare time.)

Finishing the Lesson
- Look at the page with the students, checking their answers.

97

Spelling: ‹ph› and ‹gh› Making the /f/ Sound

Spelling Test
• The students turn to the backs of their books and find the column labeled *Spelling Test 33*.
• In any order, call out the spelling words learned last week. The students write the words on the lines.

Review
• Write the following words on the board and blend and sound them out with the class: *lawn, haunt, halt, deer, mere, dear, failure, gnome, design*.
• Identify the spelling patterns: ‹aw›, ‹au›, and ‹al› saying /o/, ‹eer›, ‹ere›, and ‹ear› saying /ear/, ‹ure›, and ‹gn›.

Spelling Point
• Remind the students that they know several ways to write the /f/ sound. Ask them what they are: ‹f›, ‹ff›, ‹ph›. Explain that most words with a /f/ sound take the ‹f› spelling. However, most short words with a short vowel sound ending in /f/ take the ‹ff› spelling, as in *cliff, stuff, huff, puff,* and *off*.
• There are also a number of exceptions that take the ‹ph› spelling; these words are usually derived from Greek. Ask the students to suggest some ‹ph› words (e.g. *photo, nephew, phone, dolphin, alphabet*).
• Write some words for each spelling on the board and identify the letters making the /f/ sound.
• Now write *laugh* and *tough* on the board, and blend and sound them out with the students. Explain that a small number of words take the ‹gh› spelling, which is most often used when the /f/ sound follows a vowel at the end of a word.

Spelling List
• Read the spelling words with the students and identify the ‹ph› or ‹gh› spelling in each one. Ask the class to highlight the letters.
• Explain the meanings of any unfamiliar words.
• Point out the ‹a› saying /ai/ in *aphid*, the ‹ou› saying /u/ in *rough, toughest* and *enough*, the ‹y› in *hyphen*, the ‹s› saying /z/ in *phrase*, the ‹au› saying /a/ in *laugh* and *laughter*, the ‹i› saying /ie/ in *decipher* and *triumph*, the soft ‹c› in *decipher* and *pharmacy*, the ‹au› in *autograph*, the ‹e› saying /ee/ in *apostrophe*, the ‹i› saying /ee/ in *amphibian*, the ‹ou› saying /o/ in *coughing*, and the ‹y› saying /ee/ in *pharmacy*.

aphid
rough
hyphen
phrase
graphic
laugh
toughest
decipher
enough
phantom
autograph
apostrophe
triumph
amphibian
laughter
coughing
pharmacy
phenomenon

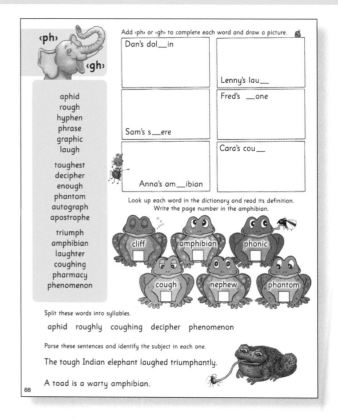

Activity Page
• The students complete each word by adding ‹ph› or ‹gh› and illustrate the word in the box.
• Next, they use a dictionary to look up the words in the amphibians. They read each definition and write the page numbers in the boxes. The students could also write a few sentences using some of the words.
• Then they identify the vowel sounds in the words and separate the words into syllables (*a/phid, rough/ly, cough/ing, de/ci/pher, phe/nom/e/non*).
• Finally, they parse the sentences and identify the subject in each one (*elephant, toad*).
The <u>tough</u> <u>Indian</u> <u>elephant</u> <u>laughed</u> <u>triumphantly</u>.
A <u>toad</u> <u>is</u> a <u>warty</u> <u>amphibian</u>.

Dictation
• Dictate the sentences below. Remind the class to use the correct punctuation in the first and second sentences. *Pam* and *Steve* are proper nouns and need capital letters.

1. "The photos of the leaping dolphins are over there," said Pam.
2. "Our little nephew can say the alphabet," said Steve proudly.
3. The elephants waved their trunks and walked off.

Grammar: Sentences and Phrases

Aim
- Refine the students' understanding of a sentence and develop their ability to tell the difference between a sentence and a phrase.

Introduction
- Review sentences. Remind the students that all sentences must make sense, start with a capital letter, contain a verb, and end with a period, question mark, or exclamation mark.
- Write the following on the board:
  ben decorated bedroom
  Ask whether this is a sentence (it is not). Ask the students what is needed to make it a sentence, and make the corrections on the board.
  ***Ben* decorated *his* bedroom.**
- Now review the subject and object of a sentence. The subject is the noun or pronoun that "does" the verb action, and the object is the noun or pronoun that "receives" the verb action.
- In the sentence on the board, draw a box around the subject, *Ben*, with a small ‹s› in the corner, and a ring around the object, *bedroom*, with a small ‹o› inside.
- Remind the students that all sentences must have a subject, but they do not necessarily have an object.

Main Point
- Now write on the board: *A treasure island.*
- Ask whether this is a sentence or not and, if not, why not. (Although it starts with a capital letter, has a period at the end, and makes sense, it is not a sentence because it has no verb and therefore no subject.)
- Explain to the students that when a group of words makes sense but has no verb it is called a phrase.
- Write the some of the following phrases on the board: *knives and forks, in the shed, today at school, at the local museum, the house next door, on the phone, out and about, a box of chocolates, in the playground, under the sea, at the hospital, the black and white cat, a Victorian house, in a few minutes, on the main road, my best friend, in the jungle, hot coffee, under the trees, long summer days.*
- Choose some of the students to read out the phrases.
- Ask the rest of the class if they can think of sentences for these phrases and write their suggestions on the board. With the class, check that they are proper sentences. Highlight the original phrase in the sentence and underline the verb in red.

Activity Page
- The students read each phrase and write it out in a sentence. They must make sure that the sentence

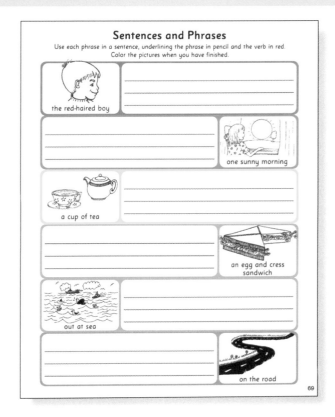

makes sense, starts with a capital letter, has a verb, and ends with a period.
- Then they underline the verb in red and the original phrase in pencil.

Extension Activity
- Provide a sheet of paper for each student. Ask the students to fold the paper in half, and then open it up again so that it has a crease running down the middle from top to bottom. They write the headings *Phrase* and *Sentence* on either side of the paper.
- Each student chooses one of the phrases from the board and copies it onto the "phrase" side, illustrating the phrase underneath. Then, they write a sentence using that phrase on the "sentence" side and illustrate their sentence underneath.

Phrase	Sentence
in the jungle	*We saw a troop of monkeys in the jungle.*
(draw a picture here)	(draw a picture here)

Finishing the Lesson
- Look at the page with the students, asking some of the students to read out one of the sentences they wrote.

Spelling: ‹air›, ‹are›, ‹ear›, and ‹ere›

Spelling Test
- The students turn to the backs of their books and find the column labeled *Spelling Test 34*.
- Call out the spelling words learned last week.

Review
- Write the following words on the board: *drawn, auburn, chalk, sniff, graph, enough, figure, gnu, dessert, desert.* Blend and sound them out with the class.
- Identify the spelling patterns: ‹aw›, ‹au›, ‹al› saying /o/, ‹ff›, ‹ph›, ‹gh› saying /f/, ‹ure›, and ‹gn›.
- Discuss the different spellings and meanings of *dessert* (pudding) and desert (abandon).

Spelling Point
- Write ‹air› on the board and ask the students what it says. Remind them that, as well as being a word, /air/ is a sound found in words like *chair* and *fairy*. (It is sometimes thought of as two sounds: an /e/ sound running into an /er/ sound.)
- Ask the students whether they know any other spellings for the /air/ sound. They may remember ‹are› and ‹ear› from the *Grammar 2 Student Book*.
- Introduce the ‹ere› spelling of /air/. Tell the students that while most words take the ‹air› and ‹are› spellings, only a few take the ‹ear› spelling, and even fewer take ‹ere› (e.g. *ere, there, where*).
- Remind them that the ‹ear› and ‹ere› spellings can also make the /ear/ sound, as in *fear* and *here*.
- Add ‹are›, ‹ear›, and ‹ere› to the board and make a short list of words for each spelling.
- Blend and sound out the words with the class, identifying the spelling of /air/ in each one.

Spelling List
- Read the spelling words with the students, identify the letters making the /air/ sound and ask the class to highlight them.
- Explain the meanings of any unfamiliar words. Point out the ‹y› in *fairy* and *dairy*, the suffixes ‹-less› and ‹-able› in *airless* and *bearable*, the prefixes ‹re-› and ‹pre-› in *repair* and *prepare*, and the ‹al› saying /o-l/ in *wherewithal*.

Activity Page
- The students read the phrases and decide which words from the spelling list they describe.
- Next, they use a dictionary to look

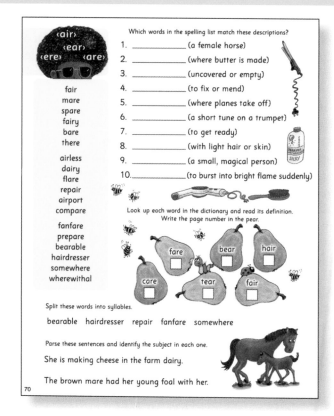

fair
mare
spare
fairy
bare
there
airless
dairy
flare
repair
airport
compare
fanfare
prepare
bearable
hairdresser
somewhere
wherewithal

up the words in the pears. They read each definition and write the page numbers in the boxes. The students could also write a few sentences using some of the words.
- Then they identify the vowel sounds in the words and separate the words into syllables (*bear/a/ble, hair/dres/ser, re/pair, fan/fare, some/where*).
- Lastly they parse the sentences and identify the subject in each one (*She, mare*). The first sentence is written in the present continuous so both parts of the verb should be underlined in red. *Farm* is a noun acting as an adjective and should be underlined in blue. In the second sentence, the first *her* is describing who owns the foal and the second *her* is taking the place of *the mare*.

She is making cheese in the farm dairy.
The brown mare had her young foal with her.

Dictation
- Dictate the sentences below. Remind the class to use the correct punctuation in the second and third sentences. *Seth* and *Meg* are proper nouns and need capital letters.

1. The bare bear had lost his hair.
2. "Can I share your pear?" asked Seth.
3. "What are you going to wear?" asked Meg.

Grammar: The Subject and Object of a Sentence

Aim
- Refine the students' ability to identify both the subject and the object of a sentence. Develop their understanding that all sentences have a subject, but not all sentences have an object.

Introduction
- Briefly review sentences and phrases. A sentence must make sense, start with a capital letter, contain a subject and verb, and end with a period, question mark, or exclamation mark. If a group of words has no verb, but makes sense when you read it, it is usually a phrase.
- Write *tasty egg sandwiches* on the board and ask one of the students to read it out. Ask the class whether it is a sentence or a phrase (it is a phrase).
- With the students, decide how it can be made into a sentence: for example, *Snake likes tasty egg sandwiches*. Write the sentence on the board and highlight the original phrase.
- Write, or call out, some more examples and ask the students whether they are sentences or phrases. When it is a phrase, ask the students to use it in a sentence.

Main Point
- Look at the sentence on the board and parse the sentence with the students, underlining the verb in red, the nouns in black, and the adjectives in blue. <u>Snake</u> <u>likes</u> <u>tasty</u> <u>egg</u> <u>sandwiches</u>.
- Point out that although the word *egg* is a noun, it is underlined in blue because it is acting as an adjective, describing (or modifying) the word *sandwich*.
- Now find the subject and object of the sentence. Remind the students that the subject is the noun or pronoun that "does" the verb action, and the object is the noun or pronoun that "receives" the verb action.
- Ask them *Who or what likes the sandwiches?* Draw a box around the word *Snake* and put a small ‹s› in the corner.
- Now ask *Snake likes what?* Draw a ring around the word *sandwiches* and put a small ‹o› inside.
- Ask the students to extend the sentence by suggesting an adverb, another adjective, or some extra information.
- Now write the following sentence on the board and ask the class whether it is a sentence or a phrase (it is a sentence). The <u>dog</u> <u>growls</u> <u>loudly</u>.
- Parse it with the students, underlining the verb in red, the noun in black, and the adverb in orange.
- To find the subject, ask the students *Who or what*

The Subject and Object of a Sentence

In each sentence, underline the verb(s) in red. Find the subject and put a box around it with a small ‹s› in the corner. Then, if there is an object, put a ring around it with a small ‹o› inside.

Zack eats an ice cream.

Rose paints a picture.

Sam runs quickly.

Lucy is riding a horse.

The dog frightened the man.

We sang happily this morning.

He crashed the car.

The dragon was breathing fire.

The author is writing a novel.

They are singing a song.

Grandpa is sleeping.

She whistles a tune loudly.

The lion climbs the tree.

The woman is taking photos.

The boy watched the monkey.

The monkey watched the boy.

When you've finished, color in the ice cream with your favorite flavors. My favorite is strawberry!

growls? Draw a box around the word *dog*, with a small ‹s› in the corner.
- Now ask whether the sentence has an object (it does not). In this sentence, there is no noun "receiving" the action of *growls*, so there is no object.
- Some of the students might say *loudly* is the object because it comes after the verb and is connected to it (in English, the order of a sentence is often subject–verb–object). If this happens, remind them that *loudly* is an adverb describing the action of the verb, whereas the object would be a noun or pronoun "receiving" the action of the verb.
- Remind the students that a sentence always has a subject, but it does not necessarily have an object.

Activity Page
- The students identify the verb in each sentence, underlining it in red. Next they find the subject of the sentence (who or what is "doing" the verb action) and draw a box around the word, with a small ‹s› in the corner.
- Then they find the object (who or what is "receiving" the action of the verb) if any. If there is an object, they draw a ring around it and put a small ‹o› inside.

Extension Activity
- The students color in the ice cream on their page.
- They write some sentences about the ice cream, making sure that they have a subject and an object.

Spelling: ‹ex›

Spelling Test
- The students turn to the backs of their books and find the column labeled *Spelling Test 35*.
- In any order, call out the spelling words learned last week. The students write the words on the lines.

Review
- Write the following words on the board: *off, phone, cough, dreary, beer, sincere, fairy, bare, bear, there, feature*. Blend and sound them out.
- Identify the spelling patterns: ‹ff›, ‹ph›, ‹gh› saying /f/, ‹ear›, ‹eer›, ‹ere› saying /ear/, ‹air›, ‹are›, ‹ear›, ‹ere› saying /air/, ‹ure›. Discuss the different spellings and meanings of *bare* and *bear*.

Spelling Point
- Review the ‹x› spelling of /ks/. When the students hear /ks/ in a word, they must decide whether they need the ‹x› spelling (e.g. *fox*) or the ‹ks› spelling (e.g. *ducks, sharks*).
- Now introduce the ‹ex› spelling, which can say either /e-ks/ or /e-gz/. Explain that ‹ex› is often a prefix. A prefix is one or more syllables added at the beginning of a word to change, or add to, the meaning.
- Write *exit, expel,* and *extract* on the board and discuss what they mean. (If you *exit* somewhere, you go out; if you *expel* something, you force it out, and if you *extract* something, you take it out of something else.) So one meaning of the prefix ‹ex› is *out* or *away from*.
- Now write *ex-dancer,* and *ex-boyfriend* on the board and discuss what the prefix means in these words (*former* or *previous*). When ‹ex› is followed by a hyphen, it usually takes this second meaning.

Spelling List
- Read the spelling words with the students and identify the ‹ex› spelling in each one. Ask the class to highlight the ‹ex›.
- Explain the meanings of any unfamiliar words.
- Point out the soft ‹c› in *except, excite,* and *excellent*, the ‹ore› spelling in *explore*, the silent final ‹e› in *expensive*, the ‹le› in *example*, the silent ‹h› in *exhibition* and *exhausted*, the ‹au› in *exhausted*, the ‹tion› in *exhibition* and *examination*, and the ‹a› saying /ai/ in *examination*.
- Discuss how the ‹s› in *excuse* says /s/ when it is a noun and /z/ when it is a verb.

exit
expect
expel
expert
extra
exist
excuse
except
explain
explore
extract
excite
excellent
expensive
example
exhibition
exhausted
examination

Activity Page
- The students put the spelling list words into alphabetical order (*examination, example, excellent, except, excite, excuse, exhausted, exhibition, exist, exit, expect, expel, expensive, expert, explain, explore, extra, extract*).
- Next, the students look up words beginning with ‹ex› in a dictionary, find six words that are not in the spelling list, and write them in the spaces provided.
- Then they identify the vowel sounds in the words and separate the words into syllables (*ex/pect, ex/pen/sive, ex/it, ex/cept, ex/cel/lent*).
- Finally they parse the sentences and identify the subject in each one (*They, expert*). The second sentence is written in the present continuous so both parts of the verb should be underlined in red.
They looked expectantly at the excellent explorer.
The excited expert is examining the expensive Roman necklace.

Dictation
- Dictate the sentences below. Remind the class to use the correct punctuation in sentences 1 and 3.

1. "Where is the exit?" she asked.
2. There was an extra seat on the bus.
3. "The experiment has exploded!" exclaimed the reporter.

Grammar: Verb Tense Tents

Aim
· Review the simple and continuous verb tenses.

Introduction
· Write *to cook* on the board and ask what sort of word it is (a verb). Remind the students that when it is in this form (e.g. *to walk, to cry, to send*) it is called the infinitive. Remind the students that verbs describe what happens in the past, present, or future, and they can be written in both simple and continuous tenses.
· Draw a simple grid on the board with three boxes across the top and two boxes down, large enough to write a simple sentence in each box. Write in the tenses as you talk about them, starting with the simple past, present, and future in the top row, and then adding the past, present, and future continuous in the bottom row.
· Discuss with the students how each tense is formed, reminding them of the rules for adding the ‹-ed› and ‹-ing› suffixes (see page 25), and pointing out where the verb *to be* is used as an auxiliary verb.
· Remind them that the simple present describes an action that is repeated or usual (e.g. *He **cooks** every day*), while the present continuous describes something that has started and is still happening (e.g. *He **is cooking** dinner*). The simple past describes an action that started and finished within a specific time (e.g. *He **cooked** a meal yesterday*), while the continuous past describes an action that had started and was still happening in the past (e.g. *He **was cooking** dinner when I called*). Similarly, the simple future describes an action which will start and finish within a specific time (e.g. *He **will cook** tonight*), while the future continuous describes an action that will start and still be happening in the future (e.g. *He **will be cooking** dinner later*).

Main Point
· Say a sentence (e.g. *I hop up and down*) and identify the verb with the class. Ask which tense it is (the simple present) and write the sentence in the simple present box in the grid.
· Call out the sentence again, using a different tense this time, and ask the students which tense box you should write it in. Continue doing this, using all six tenses, and point out the doubling rule when the suffixes ‹-ed› and ‹-ing› are added.

I hopped up and down.	(simple past)
I was hopping up and down.	(past continuous)
I hop up and down.	(simple present)
I am hopping up and down.	(present continuous)
I shall hop up and down.	(simple future)
I shall be hopping up and down.	(future continuous)

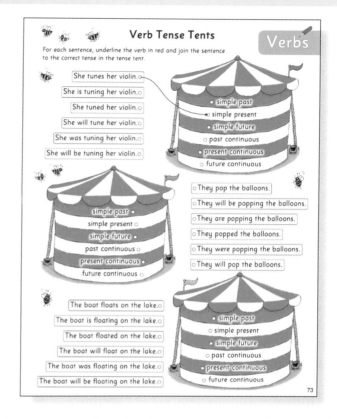

· Now say *I played with my toys* and identify the verb (*played*) and the tense (simple past) with the students. This time, call out each of the tenses in turn and ask the students how the sentence would be written in each one.

Activity Page
· The students read the sentences and decide which tense is being used in each one. They join each sentence to the correct part of the Tense Tent.

Extension Activity
· Write the following sentences on the board.
We are jumping on the trampoline.
We jumped on the trampoline.
We shall be jumping on the trampoline.
We jump on the trampoline.
We were jumping on the trampoline.
We shall jump on the trampoline.
He will be looking at the portraits.
He will look at the portraits.
He was looking at the portraits.
He looks at the portraits.
He looked at the portraits.
He is looking at the portraits.
· The students copy them out and write the appropriate verb tense next to each one.

The Grammar 4 Handbook

The teaching in *The Grammar 4 Handbook* follows on from that in the *Grammar 3 Student and Teacher's Books*. Throughout the course of this handbook, the students' understanding of language is further refined.

The students build upon their knowledge of sentence structure by learning about the difference between simple and compound sentences, and by learning how to distinguish between a phrase, a clause, and an independent clause. They also learn how to turn a statement into a question by moving the auxiliary verb to the beginning of the sentence. Regular dictation activities give the students the opportunity to practice their spelling and punctuation skills.

The students also learn new elements of grammar, including abstract nouns (such as *beauty*), infinitives (such as *to run*), possessive nouns (such as *Robert's*), and noun phrases (such as *that young brown rabbit*). In spelling, the students learn new spelling patterns like

‹or› making the /er/ sound (as in *worm*), and ‹ve› saying /v/ (as in *have*). They are also introduced to the schwa sound: the most common vowel sound in spoken English. The schwa is the sound made when the vowel in an unstressed syllable is swallowed and is pronounced /uh/. The students are also taught how to use a thesaurus in *The Grammar 4 Handbook*, with the aim of further increasing their vocabularies.

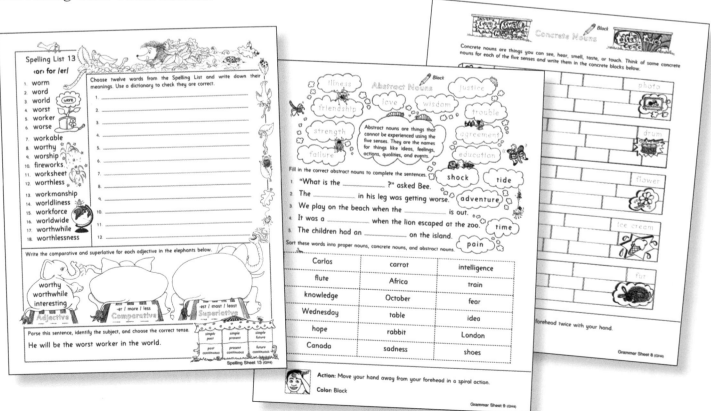